AVAILABLE
for
GOD'S
PURPOSE

AVAILABLE
for
GOD'S
PURPOSE

LESSONS FROM
THE LIFE OF ELISHA

BILL
CROWDER

Our Daily Bread
Publishing™

Requests for permission to quote from this book should be directed to: Permissions Department, Our Daily Bread Publishing, PO Box 3566, Grand Rapids, MI 49501, or contact us by email at permissionsdept@odb.org.

Scripture quotations, unless otherwise indicated, are taken from the New American Standard Bible®, Copyright © 1960, 1962, 1963, 1971, 1973, 1977, 1995 by The Lockman Foundation. Used by permission. (Lockman.org)

Scripture quotations marked KJV are from the King James Version.

Scripture quotations marked NIV are taken from the Holy Bible, New International Version®, NIV®. Copyright © 1973, 1978, 1984, 2011 by Biblica, Inc.™ Used by permission of Zondervan. All rights reserved worldwide. zondervan.com.

Scripture quotations marked NKJV are from the New King James Version®. Copyright © 1982 by Thomas Nelson. Used by permission. All rights reserved.

Interior design by Michael J. Williams, MWillustration.com

Library of Congress Cataloging-in-Publication Data

Names: Crowder, Bill, author.
Title: Available for God's purpose : lessons from the life of Elisha / Bill Crowder.
Description: Grand Rapids, MI : Our Daily Bread Publishing, [2021] |
 Summary: "Available for God's Purpose offers an amazing portrait of what
 God accomplished through the surrendered life of Elisha, and how God
 wants to do the same for all His children"-- Provided by publisher.
Identifiers: LCCN 2020050739 | ISBN 9781640700864 (paperback)
Subjects: LCSH: Elisha (Biblical prophet)
Classification: LCC BS580.E5 C76 2021 | DDC 222/.54--dc23
LC record available at https://lccn.loc.gov/2020050739

Printed in the United States of America
21 22 23 24 25 26 27 28 / 8 7 6 5 4 3 2

For our grandchildren:
Amarah, Cameron, Nathan, Henry,
Charlie, Little Buddy Bruce, Daisy, and Georgy
What a gift they are to Marlene and me!

CONTENTS

ACKNOWLEDGMENTS

I remember the moment Carol Holquist, publisher for Discovery House Publishers at the time, asked if I would be willing to write a book. I did not know then whether such a thing was even achievable for me, but I did know something with great clarity—I was going to need a lot of help.

Fifteen-plus years later that help is still required to pull off such a task, and fifteen-plus years later I continue to be grateful for the extraordinary skill, commitment, and heart that my friends and colleagues at Our Daily Bread Publishing (formerly Discovery House Publishers) willingly put into projects like this. I consider publisher Ken Petersen a friend, as I do Dawn Anderson (executive editor), Dave Branon (senior editor and wise counsel), and the ODBP marketing team of John Van der Veen and Marjie Johnson. I can't imagine trying to tackle this without you all.

I also always want to thank my family. With my first family—my parents and my siblings—during my early years each one had a part in shaping me and giving me a story to tell. In my adult life, the most influential family member I have, of course, is my wonderful wife, Marlene, who encourages me, cajoles me, and tests ideas with me all the time—especially when a project like this is on the table. To our kids and to our grandkids (to whom this book is dedicated), I can only smile and be grateful for the gift from God each one is to my heart. I am truly blessed.

To my Lord, Savior, and Shepherd, I am grateful that He was willing to be available to come to my rescue—and to give meaning and purpose to whatever availability I can offer Him. He is not only the Reason . . . He is all the reasons for a life that matters in this world. As the psalmist wisely said, ultimately, "My help comes from the LORD, who made heaven and earth" (Psalm 121:2).

WHAT GOD LOOKS FOR

The apostle Paul wasn't kidding around when he, overwhelmed by the mind and heart of a God far greater than he could ever comprehend, wrote:

> Oh, the depth of the riches, both of the wisdom and knowledge of God! How unsearchable are His judgments and unfathomable His ways! For who has known the mind of the Lord, or who became His counselor? (Romans 11:33–34)

It should be no surprise that the God who made the heavens and earth is both smarter and wiser than we are. Yet we are continually surprised by His purposes and plans. The same apostle Paul tried to grapple with that wisdom in

1 Corinthians 1:25, where he pondered: "For the foolishness of God is wiser than human wisdom, and the weakness of God is stronger than human strength" (NIV).

Primarily speaking there about the wisdom of the cross, Paul then surprises us with the amazing wisdom by which God chooses who He uses. In my book *God of Surprise*, we deal at length with what follows, 1 Corinthians 1:26–29. In Paul's words to his friends at Corinth, we discover God's radical strategy for accomplishing His work in the world.

> For consider your calling, brethren, that there were not many wise according to the flesh, not many mighty, not many noble; but God has chosen the foolish things of the world to shame the wise, and God has chosen the weak things of the world to shame the things which are strong, and the base things of the world and the despised God has chosen, the things that are not, so that He may nullify the things that are, so that no man may boast before God.

While God is clearly able to use anything (Balaam's donkey comes to mind) or anyone (including the highly gifted, highly competent, and well-trained), Paul says that "not many" of the uber-talented or highly notable end up in His grand scheme. Instead, God's masterstroke is in using the people who would, from the common perspective, seem least likely to be able to be effective. The weak. The foolish. Those who are not notable.

In order to accomplish that strategy, God tends to look primarily at something beyond pedigree, credentials, talent, or ability.

He looks for availability.

He looks for willingness, and He finds it in a fisherman willing to leave his nets, boats, and fish to follow Jesus. He finds it in a prophet who, when confronted by the greatness of God and the overwhelming nature of His mission, simply responds, "Here am I. Send me!" (Isaiah 6:8). And He finds it in a peasant girl who, upon hearing that she will be privileged to give birth to Israel's long-awaited Messiah, responds, "I am the Lord's servant. May your word to me be fulfilled" (Luke 1:38 NIV).

> *Our God searches far more for the available than for the able.*

Peter, Isaiah, and Mary show us what can be done with a willing spirit.

Our God searches far more for the available than for the able. In fact, the record of Scripture seems to make it clear that our good God delights in taking the available and *making* them able.

There was a time in the Old Testament when availability was the primary requisite—and God found that availability in a seemingly insignificant young man who was doing nothing more profound than plowing a field at his family's farm. He found it in Elisha—and in Elisha we discover an amazing portrait of what God can accomplish through an available life.

1

THE JOURNEY
BEGINS

You're traveling in the London Underground, and you pop out at the Piccadilly Circus exit by the famous Eros statue. While riding the escalators into and out of the Tube, you had seen dozens of posters promoting a new West End play starring the acclaimed actress Dame Judi Dench, and you decide to grab the opportunity to see her perform live and in person. Stopping at one of the dozens of ticket stands that clutter that part of London, you pay top price to get the best seat available.

As you settle in for the performance, you have just gotten comfortable, and it's time for the curtain to rise. However, before the play begins, an offstage voice announces, "In today's performance, the role of _____ normally played

by Dame Judith Dench will instead be played by _____."
Not Judi Dench, but her understudy. This news is usually
accompanied by a chorus of groans from the audience.

Consider for a moment the role of an understudy in a big
dramatic production. She has to be prepared and practiced
and skilled at the role she is to play—but she will only play
it if the star of the show isn't there. Talk about filling big
shoes! It's a bit uncomfortable to be the understudy. I know
that feeling.

Several years ago, I was given the challenge to fill in at
several Bible conferences for a well-known and greatly loved
Bible teacher. It was a great privilege, but it was also a daunting task—and not a little terrifying! In the first place, I knew
that I could not in any way teach the Scriptures in a way
that would replicate the winsomeness, skill, or style that had
made this teacher so beloved. In addition to that, I knew that
the people who would be attending the event were coming
in hopes of hearing him—not me. Combine those things
together, and you get a formula for potential disappointment for the people attending the conferences. *Terrifying* is
the right word for how it felt when I took the platform to a
few muffled, frustrated sighs.

Whether in science, education, sports, government, or
the arts, it can be very challenging when you have to fill
big shoes—and that is true in the Scriptures as well. There
are moments in biblical history when people are called to
fill the big shoes of their predecessors:

- Joshua led Israel into the Promised Land after Moses's
  death;
- Solomon built the temple after David's death; and

- Elisha took the prophetic role of Elijah after the first prophet was taken way in a whirlwind.

It is this last pair of predecessor and successor that we want to consider together. Elisha was called to fill the terribly big shoes of the prophet Elijah as his replacement. So, let's begin by looking at how he did and what we can learn from his story.

A Context with Concern

We enter the story during a rare time in the Bible known as an "age of miracles." We sometimes think that the Bible is shot through with miracles from cover to cover, but that is actually not so. While the Bible is infused throughout with the supernatural, it is not heavily congested with the miraculous. Although we encounter miracles from time to time in the Scriptures, there are really only three seasons in the biblical story where we see a high volume of miraculous events: the days of Moses and the Exodus, the era of Elijah and Elisha, and the times of the Gospels and Acts (more on this later).

In this study, we slot into the second of those two seasons, as the time of Elijah's miraculous ministry comes to a moment of crisis. The prophet, though in the afterglow of his greatest victory, feels his work is over. What sets the stage for this apparent resignation? This is the time of the divided kingdom. Following the death of Solomon, the two sections of Israel sever ties with one another, with the Southern Kingdom (Judah) being headquartered in Jerusalem and the Northern Kingdom (Israel) making the city of Samaria its capital. The current king of the north is Ahab, a ruler who was a brilliant engineer but a poor leader. In 1 Kings 16, we see a tragic turning point in Israel's history:

> It came about, as though it had been a trivial thing for him to walk in the sins of Jeroboam the son of Nebat, that he [Ahab] married Jezebel the daughter of Ethbaal king of the Sidonians, and went to serve Baal and worshiped him. So he erected an altar for Baal in the house of Baal which he built in Samaria. Ahab also made the Asherah. Thus Ahab did more to provoke the Lord God of Israel than all the kings of Israel who were before him. (vv. 31–33)

That's not all. Ahab's relationship with Jezebel was not only a marriage outside the parameters of Mosaic law but it was also a spiritual union that saw the institutionalized worship of the false gods Jezebel imported into Israel. Elijah the prophet became God's ultimate response in drawing His people back to himself and away from their self-destructive idolatry. After the people had endured forty-two months of drought and famine, the famous battle of the gods on Mount Carmel (1 Kings 18) resulted in the Israelites reaffirming their loyalty to the God of Abraham, Isaac, and Jacob.

While this was clearly a victory for Elijah, Jezebel was not at all pleased—and she threatened the prophet's life. That threat prompted him to run in fear, and it plunged him into a difficult time of depression as he pondered the strangeness of his life in a cave on Mount Horeb.

It is here that we enter the story. God reaches out in concern for His struggling prophet, and He begins the process of preparing Israel for life after Elijah by calling Elisha to fill those very big prophetic shoes.

A New Challenge to Consider

When we're struggling in the dark seasons of life, it can be difficult to find a way out. We can start to think that the light will never shine again. But our God is both light and life, and He enters into the darkness and death of Elijah's despair to move him forward once more. In response to Elijah's despair, God responds with provision.

First, He provides His servant with rest and nourishment (1 Kings 19:1–8), reminding us how intensely practical our Father is. Psalm 103:14 reminds us, "For He Himself knows our frame; He is mindful that we are but dust." The Father whose Son invites us to come to Him and find rest (Matthew 11:28) offers both rest and refreshment to the frightened prophet.

Part of Elijah's discouragement is rooted in the fact that he has been engaged in three and a half years of dangerous, wearying, high-profile ministry. God steps in through the angel of the Lord to give his harried prophet some much needed R & R—the military term for rest and recuperation. Make no mistake, Elijah has been in a battle, and God moves him off the front lines to let him recover from the exertions of such a challenging ministry.

Then God provides His presence to the weary prophet (1 Kings 19:9–12). After the Lord of the universe dispatches a series of natural phenomena (wind, earthquake, fire) to gain the attention of the prophet, God himself comes to Elijah in a gentle whisper. As Elijah had been fleeing from

Jezebel's wrath, he had also unwittingly distanced himself from the God who had called him and provided for him throughout the forty-two months of drought. Now, as He had done with our ancient parents who sinned in the garden in Genesis 3, God pursues the prodigal prophet and engages him in a deeply personal and intimate way. This unnerves Elijah to the point of making him try to hide from God's presence (reminiscent of Adam and Eve) by wrapping himself up in his cloak. But God will not have it, and He continues to work in Elijah's life in spite of the prophet's temporary abandonment of his call.

In the end, however, God does even more than provide for Elijah's weariness and aloneness. He also provides Elijah with a new series of tasks—a renewed purpose that will provide Israel with a new prophetic voice for decades to come.

> The LORD said to him, "Go, return on your way to the wilderness of Damascus, and when you have arrived, you shall anoint Hazael king over Aram; and Jehu the son of Nimshi you shall anoint king over Israel; and Elisha the son of Shaphat of Abel-meholah you shall anoint as prophet in your place. It shall come about, the one who escapes from the sword of Hazael, Jehu shall put to death, and the one who escapes from the sword of Jehu, Elisha shall put to death. Yet I will leave 7,000 in Israel, all the knees that have not bowed to Baal and every mouth that has not kissed him." (1 Kings 19:15–18)

God told Elijah that as part of this task, he was to perform three anointings. In the ancient world, an anointing was an act of both appointment and authority. In one sense, two of these three acts of anointing should not be surprising, for anointing kings was part of what a prophet did. Still, in all of these divinely appointed anointings there are subtle surprises that deserve our attention.

God instructed Elijah first to anoint Hazael to be king over Aram (Syria). This is shocking. Why? Because Elijah was the prophet of Israel—not Syria. It was unheard of for a Jewish prophet to anoint the king of a nation that was far more than just a rival to Israel. At this point in history, Syria was Israel's most threatening neighbor. Strange.

Second, Elijah was to anoint Jehu to be king over Israel. This gets our attention because this would make Jehu the de facto successor to the evil King Ahab. It was customary for the king's son to succeed him on the throne, but God was breaking off Ahab's line so that Jehu would rule instead of Jehoram, Ahab's son.

But it is the third anointing that really gets our attention. Elijah was to anoint Elisha to succeed him as God's prophet—and this is even more unusual. Kings and priests were anointed, but prophets normally were not. Prophets *performed* anointings; they did not receive them. Nevertheless, Elijah is instructed not only to appoint Elisha as his prophetic replacement but to anoint him as well. Then, as a part of these instructions, God informs Elijah—who thought that he alone was faithful to Jehovah—that there were seven thousand others in Israel who had not worshipped Baal.

All of these acts of God formed the Lord's provision for the battle-weary Elijah, and these provisions contained a gentle message of hope. The situation was not as dire as Elijah thought. God was still in control, and He had His people firmly in place. For Elijah, the understanding that he was not alone and that he was not quite finished must have been encouraging. It was a reminder of a very important key idea that can help us as well: God has a plan, even when we don't have a clue.

> *God has a plan, even when we don't have a clue.*

In the awareness of seven thousand faithful spiritual servants and in the anointing of Elijah's successor, God is providing comfort for His weary servant. Why? Because God's provision will meet the need of the hour. We too can trust that truth. God is here, and all is well.

A Not-So-Chance Encounter

It is no great secret that I love sports and that I am a supporter of the Liverpool Football Club of the English Premier League. The rich and storied history of the club dates back to 1892 when LFC was formed at the historic Anfield ground—where every LFC home game has been played since the club's inception.

Over the decades, LFC has produced countless footballing heroes, but among the most storied were the captains. Carrying a tremendous responsibility both on and off the field, these captains become the face of the team to the community and the voice of leadership in a match, where the captain is always identifiable by the "captain's armband" he wears on his left arm.

With the captaincy being such a demanding role, there was no small amount of consternation among Liverpool supporters when young Jordan Henderson, age twenty-four, was called upon to take over the captain's armband from club legend Steven Gerrard. Gerrard had been the consummate professional and a role model to the city as well as to the squad. How could Henderson ever live up to that high standard? For years, he seemed to struggle under the weight and expectations of the armband, but he endured. And on June 1, 2019, it was LFC captain Jordan Henderson who led his team to victory over Tottenham in club football's biggest game—the Union of European Football Associations Champions League final.

The captaincy of a football team, especially one as globally supported as the Liverpool Football Club, is a high honor. But the armband carries with it great responsibility to the club, to the team, and to the supporters. It is, in a sense, a "terrible privilege."

In much more important ways, the same would be true of the prophetic mantle that would pass from Elijah to Elisha.

> So he departed from there and found Elisha the son of Shaphat, while he was plowing with twelve pairs of oxen before him, and he with the twelfth. And Elijah passed over to him and threw his mantle on him. He left the oxen and ran after Elijah and said, "Please let me kiss my father and my mother, then I will follow you." And he said to him, "Go back again, for what have I done to you?" (1 Kings 19:19–20)

Elijah had traveled from his cave in Horeb (in the Sinai peninsula) to find Elisha. It is a journey that would take over a month to complete on foot, but at last Elijah is out of the cave and moving forward again. Even the names of the prophet and his soon-to-be protégé echo a sense of forward movement in God's work among His people: *Elijah* means "Jehovah is my God," but *Elisha* means "My God is salvation."

Elijah's name captures his mission—to remind the people that "the LORD, He is God" (1 Kings 18:39) and Baal is not. Elisha will be tasked with moving Israel forward to a greater understanding of the restoring, loving nature of the God they have once again embraced.

Following his long journey, Elijah finds Elisha near his hometown of Abel-meholah (1 Kings 19:16) in the Jordan Valley south of Bethshan and about halfway between the Dead Sea and the Sea of Kinnereth (normally known in the New Testament as the Sea of Galilee) in the Northern Kingdom of Israel. Famous for being the location of Gideon's victory over the Midianites (Judges 7:22), Abel-meholah will now be the scene of Elisha's response to the Lord's call to prophetic ministry. Again, although kings or priests were anointed for office, this is the only place where a prophet is so designated. This is unusual.

What is also intriguing is where Elijah finds his soon-to-be protégé. Classic Bible commentator Matthew Henry observed that Elisha is not at the school of prophets, or among scholars deeply embroiled in spiritual debate, or in a quiet place of prayer. He is plowing a field!

Several things make this truly informative for us:

- The fact that Elisha is plowing a field is further evidence that the forty-two-month drought and its accompanying famine are well and truly over.

- Also, Elisha must have come from a family of some means because they have twelve yoke of oxen, let alone that the fact that they had so much land that twelve yoke of oxen were required to plow it.
- It is not likely that Elisha was personally plowing with the twelve yoke of oxen. Either he was utilizing them one at a time, or more likely he was plowing with a team behind the line of eleven other teams of oxen so that there were twelve teams in all.
- He was going about his normal work, his normal business, and his normal life when God injects a new calling for his heart and future.

How does Elijah call Elisha as his replacement? Not unlike Steven Gerrard handing the armband off to Jordan Henderson, Elijah (1 Kings 19:19) "threw his mantle [cloak] on him." That cloak was not just a garment—it was an identifying mark of the prophetic office (think of John the Baptizer's camel hair clothing; Matthew 3:1–6).

If we can imagine the scene, it almost feels a bit comical. Elisha is dutifully plowing the family fields when the prophet Elijah walks into the plowed field. While it is likely that these two have never met, the facts surrounding the three years of famine and Elijah's role in that event would have spread by word-of-mouth. The result? Undoubtedly, Elisha would know Elijah both by reputation and by the prophetic cloak or mantle he wore. Without speaking a word, Elijah takes the cloak from his shoulders, throws it onto Elisha's shoulders, and keeps walking—still without saying a word!

While this practice feels rather abrupt to us, Bible scholar Adam Clarke asserted that it would have made perfect sense in that moment of history:

> Either this was a ceremony used in a call to the prophetic office, or it indicated that he was called to be the servant of the prophet. The mantle . . . was the peculiar garb of the prophet. . . . It is likely, therefore, that Elijah threw his mantle on Elisha to signify to him that he was called to the prophetic office.

It's interesting that the last time Elijah's cloak was mentioned, he was using it to hide his face from the presence and power of God. Now that same cloak becomes the instrument of calling.

Throwing a prophet's cloak around a person apparently symbolized the passing of the power and authority of the office to that individual. Elisha's reaction makes it clear that he had gotten the message—he was being called into service with Elijah.

Now we come to that critical moment. The moment where we discover Elisha's heart. He has been called—how will he answer? He is in the midst of a normal life on a normal day. Will he uproot that life to accompany Elijah? He is being challenged to accept a place in God's working among His people. Will Elisha be available?

Immediately, he shows his willingness to abandon his former life and follow the prophet. Remember, from all we can tell in the text, these two had only just met. Again, it appears that Elisha had never even seen Elijah before. In fact, when God tells Elijah to anoint him, it is the first mention of Elisha's name in the Bible. Yet the provider-God who had ministered to the hurting Elijah in the cave has prepared the way for him in the fields of Abel-meholah. With alarming obedience, Elisha is ready at that very moment to walk away from his entire life to follow the prophet.

Elisha asks for permission to say farewell to his family, and Elijah consents. The unusual reply, "What have I done to you?" (1 Kings 19:20) is an idiom meaning, "Do as you please" or "What have I done to stop you?" Elisha accepts the call, reminding us that the cloak, which is a symbol of honor, also carries the weight of responsibility—and it must be willingly accepted.

The Cost of Commitment Counted

Laozi, in chapter 64 of the *Tao Te Ching* (an ancient book of Chinese philosophy), offered one of the most practical and enduring proverbs for life: "A journey of a thousand miles begins with a single step."

For Elisha, that single step comes when he says goodbye to his family and household and prepares to follow Elijah.

So he returned from following him, and took the pair of oxen and sacrificed them and boiled their flesh with the implements of the oxen, and gave it to the people and they ate. Then he arose and followed Elijah and ministered to him. (1 Kings 19:21)

Elisha must be prepared for the task ahead, and though he will become a leader, he begins by learning to serve.

This moment of beginning, however, actually comes about with a profound ending. Remember, the large number of oxen he was plowing with signifies that Elisha comes from a family of some means. A surrender to prophetic ministry means counting the cost of walking away from what would, arguably, be an unusually comfortable life at that time in history. This vital choice is seen in things both symbolic and actual:

- **Symbolic.** Leaving Elijah, Elisha returned home to enjoy a farewell meal with his family and friends. The meat was cooked over Elisha's own plowing equipment. Thus he literally burned his past behind him (talk about burning your bridges!). From this time forward, Elisha would serve God. This break with the past is even pictured in the word *sacrificed* (v. 21), for it speaks of an act of ritual sacrifice. This is more than just a farewell bash. It is a moment of spiritual commitment, stating to his family, Elijah, and the world that Elisha is available to his God. He accepts the call to follow, serve, and learn from the prophet Elijah.

- **Actual.** Elisha became Elijah's servant, whereby he would be trained for his new prophetic office, which he would receive upon Elijah's departure.

Elisha begins a period of humble service and training at the side of the master prophet. And while God's servants (Moses, Elijah, John the Baptizer) sometimes learn in the desolation of a wilderness experience, mentorship is also a clearly biblical pattern in preparing one for spiritual service:

Joshua served under Moses.

Peter and the disciples followed Jesus.

Saul of Tarsus (Paul) was mentored by Barnabas.

Timothy and Titus learned under Paul.

So Elisha leaves home and follows the prophet—doing so at some significant personal cost. With that, this new journey begins for Elisha. The key here? Commitment to spiritual service has a cost and requires preparation—plus a willing, available heart.

> *Commitment to spiritual service has a cost and requires preparation— plus a willing, available heart.*

At the opening of this chapter, we discussed the pattern of predecessors and successors, or as I like to call them, forerunners and finishers. There are pioneers who begin a great task, and there are those who see that task to its necessary conclusion. Even here, at the beginning of Elisha's journey, we see that pattern in God's renewed call to Elijah.

It is interesting that back in the cave at Horeb, God had given Elijah three tasks. However, the first two tasks—the anointing of Hazael (2 Kings 8:15) and of Jehu (2 Kings 9)—would in fact be performed by Elisha. So what did God mean by saying that Elijah would anoint those two (1 Kings 19:15–16)? Elijah prepared the way for and passed his authority to Elisha, and in that sense he anointed Jehu and Hazael through his replacement.

Our story began with a discouraged, burned-out prophet who was ready to quit. But rather than allowing Elijah to walk away from his mission, the God of Israel instead adds a new component to it—to find, anoint, and train his successor. That successor is Elisha, and his response to Elijah's rather odd summons reveals the available heart that defines his life. His volunteering spirit and willingness to take the servant's place is echoed in the sentiment of one of Fanny Crosby lesser-known gospel songs—a song of servanthood for the believer in Jesus:

> To the work! to the work! we are servants of God,
> Let us follow the path that our Master has trod;
> With the might of His power our strength to renew,
> Let us do by His grace what He calls us to do.

May we, with God's help and strength, go and do likewise.

2

THE BIG ASK

The Free Dictionary, an online resource, defines *big ask* this way:

> "If you describe something that someone has asked you to do as a big ask, you mean that it will be difficult to do."

So, then, what does a Big Ask look like?

In sports, it may mean pushing a team to go harder in the second half than they did in the first half. In the military, the Big Ask could be a tremendously dangerous objective that a group of soldiers is being told to secure. In work, it could picture a daunting project that seems to break the barriers of legitimate possibility. In each case, what makes the Big Ask so big is the reality of our limitations. Our shortcomings make the challenge appear far greater than what our abilities can match up to.

However, in one of the great doxologies of the Bible, Ephesians 3:20–21 reminds us that because of the overwhelming capabilities of our good and great God, there is no such thing as a Big Ask with Him:

> Now to Him who is able to do far more abundantly beyond all that we ask or think, according to the power that works within us, to Him be the glory in the church and in Christ Jesus to all generations forever and ever. Amen.

We've read or heard those verses so many times that it's easy to be desensitized to them. But listen again to these amazing words.

Our God is . . .

Able to do . . .

Far more abundantly . . .

Beyond all that we ask or think . . .

That is pretty amazing, because we can ask or think a lot! Yet, no matter what our mind or imagination can conceive, it doesn't even begin to scratch the surface of the capabilities of our God. That is why, so often, our prayers sell God short. We don't really believe that God is that great or that good, so we don't really believe that He is capable of meeting the "beyond all" needs of life.

Now, just for the sake of balance, it's important to remember that when we look at this marvelous statement declaring God's glory, this is not a conversation about guaranteed outcomes or God's ultimate purposes; it is totally about His ability. God's purposes, plans, and outcomes are well and truly in His hands and left to His perfect wisdom. In no way, however, do outcomes (or the apparent lack of them) dull the wonder of the abilities of our Father. And sometimes God's determined outcomes are pretty spectacular.

Notice what happened in the Old Testament when people really bought into the ability of God:

The Red Sea was parted.
Goliath was defeated.
A widow's son was raised from the dead.
Fire fell from heaven.
The mouths of lions were held shut.

And that is just the short list. It seems that much of the time we don't even begin to reckon the ability of God, and as a result, we don't ask for Him to put that ability on display in response to our prayers. Elisha, however, was not afraid of the Big Ask, as we see next.

> *No matter what our mind or imagination can conceive, it doesn't even begin to scratch the surface of the capabilities of our God.*

In for the Long Haul

Scholars tell us that as we enter 2 Kings 2, Elijah and Elisha have been together for some seven to ten years. During that time, Elisha has learned and served and watched and participated in Elijah's ministry.

Sometimes that prophetic activity was blockbuster-esque, and other times it was quiet and restrained. Along the way, however, there was always a defined destination ahead— eventually Elijah would be leaving. Elisha's apprenticeship was a not-so-subtle hint that inevitably there would be a new prophet in town.

Now that time has arrived. It's time for Elijah to leave and Elisha to fill his sizable prophetic shoes, and that means a final journey for these two men who have walked together for the better part of a decade.

And it came about when the LORD was about to take up Elijah by a whirlwind to heaven, that Elijah went with Elisha from Gilgal. Elijah said to Elisha, "Stay here please, for the LORD has sent me as far as Bethel." But Elisha said, "As the LORD lives and as you yourself live, I will not leave you." So they went down to Bethel. Then the sons of the prophets who were at Bethel came out to Elisha and said to him, "Do you know that the LORD will take away your master from over you today?" And he said, "Yes, I know; be still."

Elijah said to him, "Elisha, please stay here, for the LORD has sent me to Jericho." But he said, "As the LORD lives, and as you yourself live, I will not leave you." So they came to Jericho. The sons of the prophets who were at Jericho approached Elisha and said to him, "Do you know that the LORD will take away your master from over you today?" And he answered, "Yes, I know; be still." Then Elijah said to him, "Please stay here, for the LORD has sent me to the Jordan." And he said, "As the LORD lives, and as you yourself live, I will not leave you." So the two of them went on.

Now fifty men of the sons of the prophets went and stood opposite them at a distance, while the two of them stood by the Jordan. Elijah took his mantle and folded it together and struck the waters, and they were divided here and there, so that the two of them crossed over on dry ground. (2 Kings 2:1–8)

While the text may read like a travelrama, it is much more. Each of the places they pass through is deeply ingrained in Israel's national memory, creating echoes of a past relationship with and provision from their God that had, for many of the people, faded into the past. *The New Bible Commentary* describes it this way:

The journey in this narrative took in places which (had) associations with Israel's past. Gilgal (1) was the first stopping-place after the Israelites had crossed the Jordan. Male Israelites born during the wilderness years were circumcised there, and a Passover was celebrated (Joshua 5). Bethel (2), some 14 miles (24 km) into the central hills, was the place of Jacob's encounter with God (Genesis 28). Jericho (4), in the Jordan valley not far from Gilgal, was the first town to fall to Joshua (Joshua 6), and the Jordan (6) had miraculously stopped to let Israel enter the land (Joshua 3).

As they go, it is apparent that the Lord was preparing the way for Elijah's departure. Part of this preparation had already happened with Elisha's anointing, but that prep work continued with God making this coming event known to both Elisha and the sons of the prophets.

On this journey, however, Elisha, the soon-to-be prophet, is caught in a verbal crossfire between his mentor, Elijah, and the sons of the prophets, a group of men that pops up periodically during the narrative. Apparently, there were prophetic schools in Israel designed to train men in the Scriptures, though they did not share the same kind of prophetic office that Elijah and Elisha occupied.

These conversations go back and forth with Elisha stuck in the middle, carrying two important themes—and those themes reveal the heart of Elisha for his mentor and friend.

The first aspect of this three-sided dialogue is found in the repeated statements from the sons of the prophets (vv. 3, 5) about Elijah's soon departure. They speak of a parting that Elisha doesn't even want to acknowledge. They persist in telling Elisha that he will soon lose his teacher and friend, and Elisha's response reveals his unhappiness at that prospect.

In Elisha's response to the prophets, according to *The Bible Knowledge Commentary,* it is as if Elisha is saying, "Do not add to my sorrow at this prospect by reminding me of it." Elisha makes it clear that he knows Elijah is leaving soon, and that awareness—coupled with his refusal to leave Elijah—seems to point to a growing sense of grief at the coming loss of his friend. It is as if Elisha can't bear the thought of losing his mentor, and he wants to hang on to him as long as possible.

I love this from Elisha, because in this moment he isn't a famous Bible character or a wonder-working prophet. He is painfully human in a way we can all identify with. Which of us hasn't been saddened at the coming departure of a friend or loved one whose absence would leave a huge vacuum in our hearts? I remember that when my father died, it felt like, in the words of a song by the Eagles, there was "a hole in the world." Certainly, there was a hole in *my* world, and it would not be easily filled. Months later, when confronted by a serious challenge or an important decision, I would instinctively pick up the phone to call Dad and ask his opinion—only to end up staring at the phone's handset in the realization that if I called he wouldn't be there. Sometimes we are defined by our successes and victories, but some of our most personal moments are defined by what we have lost. Elisha understands.

The other side of the conversation expresses Elijah's repeated requests that Elisha stay behind and Elisha's refusal to part with his friend. He does this at Gilgal, Bethel, and Jericho—the main stops along the way to the Jordan River. We don't know with certainty why Elijah kept urging Elisha to leave, but some scholars speculate that Elijah was making a kind of farewell tour to these spots with a desire to depart privately. Others think that the prophet is testing his young protégé's faithfulness. Still others suppose that he desires to spare Elisha the pain of seeing him going away permanently. But regardless of Elijah's undeclared motives behind these statements, Elisha, as the servant and student of the prophet, remains faithfully at Elijah's side.

When they arrive at the Jordan, Elijah recreates the act of Moses at the Red Sea (Exodus 14:16, 21–22). Moses's rod (shepherd's staff) was the symbol of his authority as God's appointed leader of the Hebrews. Holding that staff over the waters, Moses called upon God to create rescue— and the waters parted for the escaping former slaves to pass across to safety on the other side.

Here, Elijah uses his folded mantle, or cloak—the symbol of the prophet's divinely issued authority (1 Kings 19:19)—to strike the waters of the Jordan River in what would be his final miraculous act. As had happened centuries before with the Red Sea, the Jordan parts—enabling the two prophets to pass through.

This is but one of many parallels between the ministries of Moses and Elijah—parallels that find their culmination when these two men join together on the Mount of Transfiguration with Jesus centuries later (Matthew 17:3). *The New Bible Commentary* says, however, that this is not coincidental:

> There is a theological significance to the parallels between Elijah and Moses. Moses was the mediator of the covenant at Sinai/Horeb, the prophet (Deuteronomy 18:15; 34:10) through whom Israel was brought into that covenant relationship and made the people of God. Elijah was the prophet through whom the people were turned back to the Sinai covenant and Israel's special status was saved. H. H. Rowley neatly summed up the relationship between the ministries of Moses and Elijah: "Without Moses the religion of Yahweh as it figured in the Old Testament

would never have been born. Without Elijah it would have died."

Now Elijah's season draws to a close. The waters part for them, and they cross over to the other side, leaving the fifty sons of the prophets behind. But it is now, on the eastern side of the Jordan, that Elijah gives his student the opportunity to have a blank check—and that brings us to the Big Ask.

Up for the Big Ask

A little earlier in Israel's history, God had offered Solomon the opportunity for a Big Ask—an Ephesians 3:20–21 kind of Big Ask:

> In Gibeon the LORD appeared to Solomon in a dream at night; and God said, "Ask what you wish Me to give you." (1 Kings 3:5)

Talk about "more than you can ask or think" (see Ephesians 3:20). Offered the opportunity to make the Big Ask, Israel's new king could have asked for popularity or money or pleasure or property or a gazillion other things. He could have. But he didn't. When offered what amounted to a divine blank check, Solomon responded by declaring his great need of wisdom if he was to rule well over God's people.

Similarly, Elisha, when granted a similar offer by Elijah, asks for that which is infinitely more important than riches, fame, or greatness. In response to this gracious offer, Elisha makes the Big Ask. The "exceedingly abundantly above all" ask.

> When they had crossed over, Elijah said to Elisha, "Ask what I shall do for you before I am taken from you." And Elisha said, "Please, let a double portion of your spirit be upon me." He said, "You have asked a hard thing. Nevertheless, if you see me when I am taken from you, it shall be so for you; but if not, it shall not be so." (2 Kings 2:9–10)

As a prophet, Elijah served as God's representative before the people, so this offer has divine overtones to it—and Elisha grasps the moment with both hands. He asks for a "double portion" of Elijah's spirit, and this request for a "double portion" of Elijah's spirit has an important underlying element to it.

It is necessary to see that Elisha, like Solomon before him, declines the opportunity to seek for himself—choosing rather to request that which would equip and empower him for the challenges of the work ahead of him. Remember, Elisha has been with Elijah for years and has seen exactly what the task is and what it requires. This is a responsibility beyond him, and he knows that without divine help he has no chance of carrying the weight of this prophetic role.

It is as if Elisha were saying, "I know what this is, and I know what kind of servant of God Elijah has been. I also know what I am, and if I am to live up to this challenge, I will need twice as much of whatever God has given to Elijah!"

Faced with the Big Ask, Elisha's request is one of humility and self-awareness. And it shows that through his years of serving as Elijah's assistant, he has developed the heart of a servant.

To our ears this request for a "double portion" may not seem like such a huge thing, but Elijah himself puts it in perspective, saying, "You have asked a hard thing" (2 Kings 2:10). This is a massive request! And Elijah informs him that it will only happen if Elisha witnesses his coming departure—a departure that would be nothing less than spectacular!

> As they were going along and talking, behold, there appeared a chariot of fire and horses of fire which separated the two of them. And Elijah went up by a whirlwind to heaven. Elisha saw it and cried out, "My father, my father, the chariots of Israel and its horsemen!" And he saw Elijah no more. Then he took hold of his own clothes and tore them in two pieces. (2 Kings 2:11–12)

Sometimes when this story is told, it is said that Elijah left the world in a fiery chariot, but that isn't so. The prophet left the world in the whirlwind, of which *The Bible Knowledge Commentary* says, "The whirlwind was actually a storm with lightning and thunder. Like the pillar of cloud that led the Israelites in the wilderness (Exodus 13:21), it represented God's presence." Apparently, the chariot and horses of fire were there to separate Elijah from Elisha. What's this all about?

In our day, we have extraordinary military technologies with things like so-called "smart" bombs. Troops employ high-tech gear such as night-vision goggles that turn the darkness of light into the clarity of near-daylight. Unmanned drones fly high in the sky, creating both a safety net to protect troops from danger and serious questions about the morality of drone warfare. These instruments of war and countless others like them constitute the cutting edge of military capabilities in the modern world.

In the ancient world, however, chariots formed the leading edge of military technology. Providing speed and mobility of an unprecedented nature, chariots had developed into the most fearsome tool in an army's arsenal. And the more chariots an army had, the more likely it was that they would prevail in combat.

With that in view, Elisha's words display a conviction that Elijah, as God's representative, had served as Israel's national security during his tenure as prophet. As such, the chariot of fire and horses of fire point to an even higher, greater, and more powerful force. Elijah was being summoned to the presence of the God whose power far exceeded any might known to this world. And the same God who was so dramatically calling His servant home was also installing Elisha to represent this power in the world of his day.

Not only does Elisha witness Elijah's departure but he also feels the weight of it emotionally as he cries out to his spiritual "father" in grief. Overwhelmed by both the sight and the loss it represented, Elisha tears his clothing—the ancient Jewish symbol of grief, loss, or repentance.

Over to You, Elisha

When I was in Bible college, I played on our intercollegiate soccer team. The American in me meant that I would of necessity be a goalkeeper—I just had to use my hands! I was trained and coached continually by Seth Afari, a Ghanaian who had played goalie his entire life but would be playing as striker for us. He taught and I tried to learn; he coached and I tried to apply. He urged, cajoled, yelled, and encouraged, and I tried to not make a mess of it. Practice and training was one thing, but the first actual match was something else.

Since goalkeepers are the only players allowed to use their hands, they wear a different-colored jersey than the rest of the team or than that of the opposition. The first time I put on that game shirt and jogged out onto the pitch for pregame warm-ups, that shirt felt infinitely heavier than the mere cloth from which it had been made. It carried the weight of responsibility, reminding me that I was the last line of defense: If I didn't allow the opposition to score, we couldn't lose. I was no mere bystander. I had *the* shirt.

I wonder if a similar sense of weighty responsibility was on Elisha's mind as he watched his spiritual father and friend ascend in the whirlwind. I especially wonder if he felt that burden as he looked down and at his feet saw Elijah's prophetic mantle—the same mantle that had briefly fallen upon him years earlier. This was a defining moment for Elisha. The proverbial fork in the road. Would he return home to Abel-meholah and go back to farming, or would he, with clear knowledge of the burden it represented, pick up the prophetic mantle (cloak) that Elijah had left behind and assume the role for which he had spent these years training?

> He also took up the mantle of Elijah that fell from him and returned and stood by the bank of the Jordan. He took the mantle of Elijah that fell from him and struck the waters and said, "Where is the LORD, the God of Elijah?" And when he also had struck the waters, they were divided here and there; and Elisha crossed over. Now when the sons of the prophets who were at Jericho opposite him saw him, they said, "The spirit of Elijah rests on Elisha." And they came to meet him and bowed themselves to the ground before him. (2 Kings 2:13–15)

Ever since the day Elijah had tossed this same cloak across Elisha's shoulders, the future had been theoretical. It was "out there." But that was no longer the case. Now it was very present and very real. It is one thing to be available when that availability isn't put to the test. But now the test was here in full force.

I can only imagine the questions that might have swirled through Elisha's heart and mind:

Why couldn't Elijah have stayed longer?
Am I really ready?
Can I actually do this?
And perhaps most of all . . .
Will I receive that double portion of enabling that I requested?

The answer came as Elisha, while carrying the prophetic mantle of his mentor, approached the banks of the Jordan River he had crossed with Elijah just moments earlier. Would Elisha's willingness and availability be supported by God's matchless power and ability? Had the God of Elijah responded to the Big Ask of Elisha?

I love what the Bible teacher Warren Wiersbe (1929–2019) wrote:

> Elisha took Elijah's mantle (see 1 Kings 19:19) and dared to trust God for the power to do the impossible. It was one thing to cross Jordan with Elijah, but quite another to step out by faith by himself. But when you trust "the Lord God of Elijah," you do not need Elijah too.

There it is.

Elisha's resulting ministry would be as strong a contrast to that of Elijah as was the difference between the ministries of Moses and Joshua, and ultimately even the differences separating the roles of John the Baptist and Jesus. British theologian A. W. Pink (1886–1952) wrote:

> The first miracle performed by Elisha was identical with the last one wrought by his master: the smiting of the waters of the Jordan with the mantle, so that they parted asunder for him (2 Kings 2:8, 14). At the beginning of his ministry Elijah had said unto Ahab king of Israel, "As the Lord God of Israel liveth, before whom I stand" (1 Kings 17:1 KJV). And when Elisha came into the presence of Ahab's son he also

declared, "As the Lord of hosts liveth, before whom I stand" (2 Kings 3:14 KJV). As Elijah was entertained by the widow of Zarephath and rewarded her by restoring her son to life (1 Kings 17:22), so Elisha was entertained by a woman at Shunem (2 Kings 4:8–10) and repaid her by restoring her son to life (2 Kings 4:35–37). The first miracle of Elijah was that for the space of three and a half years there should be neither dew nor rain according to his word, whereas the first public act of Elisha was to heal the springs of water (2 Kings 2:21, 22) and to produce an abundance of water (2 Kings 3:20). One of the most noticeable features of Elijah's life was his loneliness, dwelling apart from the apostate masses of the people; but Elisha seems to have spent most of his life in the company of the prophets, presiding over their schools. The different manner in which their earthly careers terminated is even more marked: the one was taken to heaven in a chariot of fire, and the other fell sick in old age and died a natural death.

In both cases, however, God would continue to speak and work among His people. Elijah's ministry of aggression and strength would be followed by Elisha's more compassionate approach (in most situations). God's heart was being revealed to His people through both prophets. And central to that revealing was Elisha's willingness to request something beyond imagination—a double portion of power. It is a willing heart that echoes the words of songwriter Frances Havergal, who wrote:

Take my life, and let it be
Consecrated, Lord, to Thee;
Take my moments and my days,
Let them flow in ceaseless praise,
Let them flow in ceaseless praise.

3

WATER, WATER EVERYWHERE

In his epic 1798 poem *The Rime of the Ancient Mariner,* Samuel Taylor Coleridge penned these words:

> Water, water, every where,
> And all the boards did shrink;
> Water, water, every where,
> Nor any drop to drink.

The poem speaks of the dangers faced by ships at sea—many of those dangers coming from the sea itself. Here, specifically, Coleridge captures the desperation of sailors stuck at sea without wind to push them on, surrounded by water they can't drink.

Because it is absolutely necessary to life, water is one of the most coveted elements on earth. But it is also one of the most dangerous. Sometimes it's dangerous because there's too much of it—as was seen in the horrific devastation of the 2004 Indian Ocean tsunami, the 2005 Hurricane Katrina in New Orleans, or the 2019 Hurricane Dorian in the Bahamas. Massive walls of water crashed down on cities and homes, displacing people and disrupting lives—creating waves of desperation in the hearts of those affected.

On the opposite end of the spectrum, there are areas in the world where the problem is a serious shortage of water. Places where people walk hours each way just to get enough water to make it through the day. Places where there is no water at all.

In still other places, there is plenty of water but it isn't potable—like the Ancient Mariner's problem. Drinking a small amount of bad water can make you deathly ill—as I experienced on a teaching trip several years ago.

It was the morning of my long journey home (some thirty hours of flying and transit) after a long, three-week trip. For the entire trip, I had been extremely careful about only drinking bottled water and even brushing my teeth with the bottled stuff. But on that last morning, distracted by packing and preparations for travel, I absent-mindedly rinsed my toothbrush in tap water and put it in my mouth. That was all it took. I was terribly ill the entire thirty hours of travel back to the States and even for several days beyond that. It was a brutally painful lesson in how problematic bad water can be.

Water is perpetually integrated into the biblical story—in part because of its importance to life in general but also because of its impact on an agrarian culture. The more closely connected a people are to the land, the more aware they will be of water problems. Perhaps that is why there are so many water-related miracles in the Scriptures.

Moses (whose name, ironically, means "drawn from the water") had much to do with water miracles. In his confrontations with Pharaoh, he saw the Nile River turned to blood. And in the Hebrew people's exodus from Egypt, he witnessed the power of God in splitting the Red Sea so the Israelites could cross on dry land. Three days into the Sinai wilderness, they encountered a pool of poisoned water that was made pure when a dead tree was cast into it. Moses also saw water drawn from a rock twice—once when he spoke to the rock and once when he struck it.

As the children of Israel prepared to enter the Promised Land, Joshua led the people through the parted waters of the Jordan River and into their new home.

Elijah's prayers saw the rain withheld and then released again three and a half years later—with the pivot point in that drought/famine being the battle of the gods on Mount Carmel. There, fire fell from heaven and consumed a sacrifice and the altar that it rested upon. That altar, by the way, had been soaked by twelve jars (some translations say *barrels*) of water—completely drenching the sacrifice and stones. Elijah's final miracle, as we have seen, was to reverse Joshua's act as he exited the land of Israel by splitting the Jordan River.

And we shouldn't forget that Elisha's first miracle was the mirror image of Elijah's final wonder—splitting the Jordan so the new prophet could reenter the land.

Water's high-profile presence in the Scriptures continues on into the New Testament. Jesus's first miracle was to transform water into wine, and among other miraculous events concerning water, He actually strolled across the Sea of Galilee. Water, water everywhere, indeed.

An Interesting Context

Moving forward in Elisha's story, the first thing we need to do is to connect this event to where we were in the previous chapter. Elisha, following Elijah's impressive departure from this earth, asked the God of Elijah to give him a double portion of Elijah's "spirit." As we have seen, he was not asking to be twice as famous or to perform double the number of miracles that God had done through Elijah. Yet, God did exactly that—*exactly*. Elijah was God's instrument for eight recorded miracles, while Elisha performed sixteen! Notice:

- **Elijah** stopped the rain with his prayers; multiplied oil and grain for the widow of Zarepheth during the three and a half years of drought-induced famine; raised that same widow's son from the dead; called fire from heaven; prayed for the rains to return; called for fire to rain down on fifty-one soldiers; called for fire to fall down on fifty-one *more* soldiers; parted the Jordan River en route to his departure to heaven.

- **Elisha** parted the Jordan River using Elijah's cloak; healed the poisoned waters of Jericho; summoned bears from the woods to attack his tormenters; provided water for kings; provided oil for a widow; gave a barren woman the gift of a son; raised that same child from the dead; healed a poisoned stew; multiplied bread for the hungry; healed Naaman of his leprosy; smote Gehazi for his deceitfulness; caused a lost axe head to float so it could be recovered; gave sight to the blind, then struck other men with blindness; restored their sight once more; resurrected a dead man who touched Elisha's dead bones.

As we have seen, in the cases of both Elisha and Elijah, a significant number of their miracles involved water. And so it would be with Elisha's first two miracles. First (as we saw in the previous chapter), Elisha parted the Jordan River as Elijah had done. After the young prophets-in-training fruitlessly searched for Elijah, Elisha heads to Jericho (2 Kings 2:18)—the first major city on the west side of the Jordan. Jericho was the site of Israel's first important victory during the time of Joshua's conquests (Joshua 6), and now it once again is placed on center stage of the biblical drama.

In our day, most study trips to Israel include a stop at Jericho. It is a lovely West Bank oasis in the middle of the desert, and it offers tourists restaurants, shopping for souvenirs, and, for a price, the obligatory camel ride (those camels spit and bite!). But Jericho actually carries a significance far more important than simply being a tourist trap. It is one of the oldest cities in the world. For some perspective, consider this:

- The United States is less than 250 years old.
- A number of years ago, I was in Moscow as Russia celebrated the 800th birthday of their capital.
- A couple of years later, I was in Jerusalem during the celebration of the city's 3,000th birthday.

However, some historians believe that Jericho could be as much as 8,000 years old, making it one of the oldest cities in the world! Why has Jericho endured? Because of its natural spring, providing an abundance of fresh water.

In the ancient world, three issues were critical when looking for a location to build a new city. First, the site had to be in a place that could be defended against attack. This often meant that a city (Jerusalem, for instance) would be built on a high place where danger could be seen from all directions. Second, the city would need to be near a trade route so business and commerce could succeed, providing income for the residents of the town. Third, there needed to be an ample freshwater supply.

Jericho's fresh water spring (sometimes called Ain-es-Sultan, "The Sultan's Spring") had been a useful water source for the community for centuries. It created a fertile, crop-producing belt in the midst of an otherwise barren place that would also become a hub of economic activity on the west side of the Jordan River.

In Elisha's time, however, that had changed dramatically. The people of Jericho were experiencing a water problem. And the problem there had more in common with my bad-water experience than with those who battle with too much or too little water. Second Kings 2:19–22 tells us that the once-pristine water supply had become poisonous.

An Implied Request

In one of the earliest events in Jesus's public ministry, the Master encounters a Roman centurion whose young servant is fatally ill. The man was desperate for Jesus's help. The combined accounts from Matthew's and Luke's gospels show the soldier first sending a delegation of Capernaum's synagogue leaders to Jesus, followed by some of his friends (perhaps other Romans?). Finally, the centurion himself approaches Jesus seeking His intervention for the beloved servant. What is odd about this is that despite all of that effort to secure Jesus's help, when the centurion finally appears before Jesus he doesn't even voice a request. He merely announces that the boy is ill. In spite of the desperate nature of the situation, the request for the boy's healing (which Jesus would supply) is left implied.

This kind of restrained desperation is seen as the leaders of Jericho seek Elisha's help. Notice that while they articulate the nature of their problem they—like the Roman centurion standing before Jesus—don't actually voice a request:

> Then the men of the city said to Elisha, "Behold now, the situation of this city is pleasant, as my lord sees; but the water is bad and the land is unfruitful." (2 Kings 2:19)

Clearly, these civic leaders are approaching Elisha for his help, and they give him an analysis of the size of the challenge they face. This Jericho was a massive paradox—the location for the city is ideal and one that should be promising, but they have a water problem. And that problem is extreme to say the least. The unfruitfulness of the land appears to be connected to the bad water.

But there is more. Elisha's declaration in verse 21 says that both death and unfruitfulness were impacting the community due to the poisoned spring. In verse 19, the word *unfruitfulness* is directly applied to the land, but in verse 21 it is connected to death. For this reason, the Hebrew word here is translated in the English Standard Version as *miscarriage*. Not only were the crops being impacted by the bad water but pregnant women were miscarrying their babies because of it as well. The legitimate concern of poor crops and the uncertainty that generated regarding the future was easily trumped by the grief and pain of those who had lost children because of the situation.

Clearly, the situation the leaders of the city laid before Elisha is serious. And because he was a prophet, their statement carries with it an implied request that he do something about it. This expectation was not common for Israel's prophets. Most had a primarily spoken ministry, and some were "writing prophets." Few, however, were engaged in the miraculous. So, why would they come to Elisha with such a dramatic request?

First, Elisha had apprenticed under Elijah, who was widely known for the expressions of the miraculous that accompanied his ministry. As we saw earlier, the profound list of wonders God accomplished through Elijah could easily have caused the expectation of the miraculous to attach itself to Elijah's student/protégé/successor, Elisha.

Second, the sons of the prophets, whom Elisha had encountered upon his return across the Jordan (v. 15), were witnesses of his replication of Elijah's crossing. They recognized that Elijah's prophetic mantle had quite literally fallen to Elisha. And they saw that "The spirit of Elijah rests on Elisha." With those witnesses available, it is not hard to imagine that before seeking Elisha's help, the city leaders had received a report from those young men of what they had seen Elisha doing.

This validation was apparently enough to convince them to go to the brand-new prophet of Israel for help on, for all intents and purposes, his first day on the job. The "sons of the prophets" had no doubt already validated Elisha's prophetic appointment by witnessing his first miracle. Now the people of Jericho desperately needed the prophet's second miracle which, like the first, involved water. And not surprisingly, Elisha makes himself available.

An Ironic Response

The older I get and the longer I study the Scriptures, the more convinced I am that there is a heavy dose of mystery sprinkled throughout this divinely inspired book. There are so many head-scratching things to ponder in the biblical story that I find myself repeatedly retreating to Isaiah's record of God's comforting words—words that routinely find their way into my teaching and writing:

> "For My thoughts are not your thoughts,
> Nor are your ways My ways," declares the
> LORD.
> "For as the heavens are higher than the
> earth,
> So are My ways higher than your ways
> And My thoughts than your thoughts."
> (Isaiah 55:8–9)

> *I can trust that He will always accomplish His purposes in the ways He knows best—even if they don't make sense to us.*

In what way are those words comforting? I find them comforting because they remind me that my God doesn't need to explain himself to me. In some ways, His works and wisdom may be counterintuitive, at times even confusing, but all is well. I can trust that He will always accomplish His purposes in the ways He knows best—even if they don't make sense to us. Okay . . . even if they don't make sense to me.

This sense of counterintuitive mystery in God's working can be seen in Elisha's method for healing the Jericho spring:

> He said, "Bring me a new jar, and put salt in it." So they brought it to him. He went out to the spring of water and threw salt in it and said, "Thus says the LORD, 'I have purified these waters; there shall not be from there death or unfruitfulness any longer.'" (2 Kings 2:20–21)

I love salt. I love it on french fries and burgers and mashed potatoes and chicken and American fried potatoes and corn on the cob and hash brown potatoes and, well, you get the idea. I like potatoes, but I especially like the salt that gives them flavor. In fact, my wife Marlene is pretty sure I like salt too much. But it tastes good.

As we know, physical work or intense athletic competition causes us to sweat out the salt that is needed to keep our physical bodies operational. The salt we lose in sweat needs to be replenished if we are to be healthy.

And salt works as an excellent preservative for meat. While the practice of salting beef or pork was more prevalent during the years before the arrival of refrigeration, still today there are few things tastier than a good, salt-cured Virginia ham. Did I mention that I like salt?

However, with all the value we find in salt, it can also cause problems. In the film *Unbroken*, we find World War II Army Air Corps bombardier Louis Zamperini and two fellow servicemen whose plane ditches in the ocean. They drift across the vast Pacific in a life raft—surrounded by water they cannot drink because of the high salt content. Again, "water, water every where, nor any drop to drink." Similarly, the high mineral and salt content of the Dead Sea is so deadly that swallowing less than a cup of water can be fatal. While salt can do a lot of things, it doesn't necessarily help water.

So, in a counterintuitive process, God's servant throws salt on the poisoned spring to cleanse it. Talk about mystery. Elisha throws a contaminant into contaminated water in hope of un-contaminating it.

Add to that, this water supply is a natural spring, which would seem to indicate that the problem is at the source of the spring. How could sprinkling some salt on the *surface* solve a problem that is occurring at the *source*? Is it possible that God's higher thoughts and higher ways (Isaiah 55) are being represented in Elisha's salt-sprinkling adventure?

So, then, what is going on here?

This miracle reminds us afresh of how often the work of God is done in a way that reveals the power of mystery. How many times do we see Jesus, the king of an upside-down kingdom, do things in ways that seem the opposite of what would be logical or reasonable?

- He healed a man's congenital blindness by packing his eyes with mud (John 9);
- He proved His own majesty and greatness by living in humility and servanthood (Philippians 2);
- He reminded us repeatedly that leadership in the kingdom is best utilized by those who come from the lowest place;
- He provided life for us through the means of His own death (John 3:16); and
- He spoke of the narrowness of the kingdom way, but He clearly demonstrated that that narrow way is wide enough for the sinner, the broken, and the marginalized.

He is the One whose grace proves that our only hope of strength comes when we embrace the facts of our weakness and frailty (2 Corinthians 12).

Using something that pollutes (in this case, salt) to purify is an Old Testament example of the work of a God whose ways are higher than our ways and whose thoughts are higher than our thoughts. But counterintuitive or not, God's provision for the people of Jericho was effective and in this case immediate!

An Instantaneous Result

We live in the age of the immediate, an influence that feeds our craving for instant gratification. When my wife and I watch home improvement shows on television, we talk about how long it takes to design the new layout of the house project at hand. How long it takes to do the demolition. How long it takes to rewire electrical, rerun plumbing, rebuild walls, reinstall cabinets. It is a process that, depending on the project, can last months. But we get the entire makeover condensed into a thirty-minute package, minus commercials. The whole thing is an exercise of instant gratification for us, although it was highly delayed for the homeowners eager to get into their exciting new domicile.

Elisha's makeover of Jericho's water supply was instantaneous:

> He went out to the spring of water and threw salt in it and said, "Thus says the Lord, 'I have purified these waters; there shall not be from there death or unfruitfulness any longer.'" So the waters have been purified to this day, according to the word of Elisha which he spoke. (2 Kings 2:21–22)

Of greatest importance here is not the immediacy of the result, however. It is the clear statement by Elisha that while he was the agent of God's provision, it was God himself who had come to their aid. It was God himself who had solved their problem.

The healing of the spring was clearly an important moment for this community. But there is something else at work here as well. Throughout Elijah's prophetic ministry, Israel lapsed into idolatry by worshipping Baal—the god of fertility who was supposed to protect the crops of his devotees. Where was Baal? He clearly was not showing his supposed ability to make the ground yield crops. No, it is

Israel's God of rescue who did that. The God of Abraham, Isaac, and Jacob. The God they had repeatedly abandoned for the gods of the nations. This is the God who could and in fact *did* come to their aid. And the surprising means of accomplishing the act of cleansing for Jericho's spring showed that it was not a moment of human invention. It was an event of divine intervention. And it took effect immediately.

An Important Pattern

We've been considering this event from up close, but let's expand our view for a moment. Having been in clear sight of the trees, we need to pull back for a glimpse of the forest—the big idea behind this small story.

Everything in the Bible— either in the Old Testament or the New Testament— points us to Jesus.

If we see this act as part of the bigger story of the Bible (something we will explore more fully in chapter 6), we can see how the water miracles in the wilderness and in the land itself give a hint of the One who would come. One who would also do much with water.

I don't think it's too much to say that everything in the Bible—either in the Old Testament or the New Testament—points us to Jesus. Yes, this event does have its roots solidly grounded in history with actual people living their daily lives with its struggles and with its ups and downs. So it has its own significance and its own importance; therefore, it has its own value.

But there is more. All of the "little" stories of the Bible point to a larger story: The Bible's big story. The greatest story ever told. Each of these "little" stories, while having their own impact and influence on the generation involved, point to the ultimate divine intervention when God would send His Son to rescue His lost and broken world. In that way, each story either points directly to Jesus or exposes the fallenness of our hearts and why we need Him so much. So how might this story from Elisha's life point us to Jesus? I would suggest a couple of possibilities.

First, remember Joshua's encounter with Jericho in Joshua 6. After conquering this major city, Joshua did something quite unusual—he pronounced a curse upon Jericho:

> Then Joshua made them take an oath at that time, saying, "Cursed before the LORD is the man who rises up and builds this city Jericho; with the loss of his firstborn he shall lay its foundation, and with the loss of his youngest son he shall set up its gates." (Joshua 6:26)

This curse, some scholars believe, was at the root of the water problem at Jericho—because the people there were living in a city that should never have been rebuilt. But rather than extending the curse declared by Joshua, Elisha heals the water, lifting the curse and affirming Jericho's renewed existence.

In a far more significant way, Jesus's mission on the cross included Him bearing and taking away *our* curse. Paul, in an extremely dense passage, explained this to the Galatian followers of Christ:

For as many as are of the works of the Law are under a curse; for it is written, "Cursed is everyone who does not abide by all things written in the book of the law, to perform them." Now that no one is justified by the Law before God is evident; for, "The righteous man shall live by faith." However, the Law is not of faith; on the contrary, "He who practices them shall live by them." Christ redeemed us from the curse of the Law, having become a curse for us—for it is written, "Cursed is everyone who hangs on a tree"—in order that in Christ Jesus the blessing of Abraham might come to the Gentiles, so that we would receive the promise of the Spirit through faith. (Galatians 3:10–14)

This is a story in motion, and it is moving toward an ultimate goal. Elisha overturning the curse placed by Joshua brought the story of Jericho forward, and it encourages us to look forward beyond Elisha to the One Person that pastor Tim Keller would call "the truer and better Joshua" and "the truer and better Elisha." To lift our eyes in anticipation of the ultimate Joshua/Elisha—Yeshua, Jesus—who lifted our curse as He bore our sins in His own body on the tree.

Second, in John 4 Jesus encountered a woman at a well where He asked for a drink . . . of water. After a lively discussion about men and women, religious controversies, and natural thirst, Jesus said to her:

"If you knew the gift of God, and who it is who says to you, 'Give Me a drink,' you would have asked Him, and He would have given you living water." (John 4:10)

And . . .

> Jesus answered and said to her, "Everyone who drinks
> of this water will thirst again; but whoever drinks of
> the water that I will give him shall never thirst; but
> the water that I will give him will become in him
> a well of water springing up to eternal life." (John
> 4:13–14)

Not only does Jesus remove our curse through His work
on the cross but He also makes available to us the living
water that can fully, thoroughly, and eternally satisfy our
thirsty hearts.

This imagery of water—our dependence on it and the
Bible stories about it—anticipates the Christ. Jesus would
come as the One who would be baptized in water, would
wash His disciples' feet with water, would walk on water,
and would declare himself to be true source of Living Water.
As Moses sweetened the waters of Marah with a tree, and as
Elisha purified the poisoned waters of Jericho with salt, the
day would come when Jesus would use His very first miracle—don't miss this—to show His power to not just sweeten
water but to also turn water into wine (John 2).

That is why He is not just the Savior who forgives our
sins and lifts our curse. Jesus is also the One who quenches
our thirsty hearts with living water. No wonder, then, that
as the book of Revelation winds down, the ultimate invitation is offered to the reader:

> The Spirit and the bride say, "Come." And let the one
> who hears say, "Come." And let the one who is thirsty

come; let the one who wishes take the water of life without cost. (Revelation 22:17)

Songwriter G. R. H. Wood echoed this thought when he wrote:

> Rivers of living water
> Rivers that flow from the throne,
> Rivers o'erflowing with blessing,
> Coming from Jesus alone.
> Rivers of living water,
> Rivers of life so free,
> Flowing from Thee, my Savior,
> Send now the rivers through me.

4

REACHING
BEYOND

They say that confession is good for the soul, so here goes: I am a smart aleck. I don't think sarcasm is a spiritual gift, but if it were, it would probably be mine. In the very least, the wisecrack is hardwired into my DNA. That wiring was enhanced when, as a boy, I was exposed to things like *The Cynic's Quotebook, Mad's Snappy Answers to Stupid Questions,* and the "B.C." comic strip's infamous character Curls, "the master of sarcastic wit." Such literary treasures (see, that was sarcasm right there) fed my tendency for the smart remark, and they equipped me to seemingly always have a comment for every time or situation. A wisecrack for all seasons, as it were.

Now, why am I telling you all of this? I have to confess that if confession is supposed to be good for the soul, that one didn't help much. But it did remind me of a word that I learned to really dread as a kid. A word that my father leveled at me often. A word that was his go-to response to my sarcastic remarks. When I had just scythed through someone with a less-than-kind comment, my dad would look at me with laser-like intensity and simply say, "Attitude." Sometimes he would follow that with, "Watch your attitude" or "Mind your attitude," but the import of the comment was always the same—my words were betraying an attitude that was not very wholesome.

As a result, I grew up really hating the word *attitude*, and when I became a follower of Christ, I found that my dad wasn't alone in his concern for my attitude. The apostle Paul wrote, "Have this attitude in yourselves which was also in Christ Jesus" (Philippians 2:5). Now this attitude thing was being taken to the ultimate level of the example of Jesus—whose heart attitude was one of selflessness, self-sacrifice, and servanthood (vv. 6–8). A far cry from sarcasm and smart remarks, Jesus's attitude was one of concern for others and compassion for their brokenness.

The bottom line? Attitude matters. And that brings us back to Elisha. As we move forward in his story, we now arrive at perhaps his most well-known moment—the healing of Naaman the leprous military leader. Neatly contained within this fascinating event are some equally fascinating attitudes that at times reflect the attitude of Christ and at other times make me hear the echo of my dad's voice saying, "Watch your attitude."

As Bible teacher Chuck Swindoll wisely noted, "We cannot change our past. We cannot change the fact that people act in a certain way. We cannot change the inevitable. The only thing we can do is play on the one string we have, and that is our attitude."

So let's reenter Elisha's story and see a particular event where we can listen to a variety of people play that one string—and hear the note their attitude produces.

Naaman: An Attitude of Desperation

> Now Naaman, captain of the army of the king of Aram, was a great man with his master, and highly respected, because by him the LORD had given victory to Aram. The man was also a valiant warrior, but he was a leper. (2 Kings 5:1)

That is where the story begins, but for us it might be wise to start with some historical context. Aram (which is modern-day Syria) was a burgeoning empire to the northeast of the Northern Kingdom of Israel. It was also one of greatest, if not *the* greatest, of Israel's enemies at this moment in history. As we shall see, that adds some particular spice to the description of Naaman. Who was he?

Most notably, Naaman was a brilliant military leader. His rank was "captain of the army of the king of Aram," which would have been a very high rank, perhaps even paralleling the position of a modern general. Not only did he have a high position in Syria's military but Naaman also had a track record of success. He is described as:

A great man with his master

Highly respected

A valiant warrior

High praise, indeed! Naaman had earned the admiration of his king, Ben-hadad II, whose rule over Syria/Aram some scholars date from 864–841 BC (more on the king later). Yet the narrator, in the midst of giving us a brief résumé of Naaman's accomplishments, drops on us a tantalizing little piece of data: The victories that Naaman had enjoyed—particularly over Aram/Syria's near enemy, Israel—were not simply the result of his valor, his strategy, or his ability to inspire the troops (and the king). Notice this surprising phrase from 2 Kings 5:1: "by him the LORD had given victory to Aram."

Immediately, I want to shout, "Time out! Aram is Israel's enemy. How can Israel's God be giving victory to Israel's enemy?" I believe that to be a legitimate question. It is nothing short of shocking to think that Israel's enemy would receive the aid and assistance of Israel's God—until you bring the larger history of God's dealing with His people into focus.

Throughout Israel's sojourn as the people of God, they were constantly on the edge of abandoning God for the idols of the surrounding pagan nations. Often, as in the days of Elijah, they in fact *did* walk away from the God of their fathers to worship idols of stone, bronze, or gold made by the hands of men. When those seasons of spiritual adultery flared, God would often use one of the surrounding nations as His instrument of discipline to correct His people and draw them back to himself. This saw the Philistines as God's tool of correction in the days of the judges, and it saw the Babylonians as that disciplinary device during the prophetic career of Jeremiah. Here, Aram/Syria is functioning in that role, with Naaman experiencing victory over Israel because God was allowing it. The loving Father was correcting His wayward children through a most fascinating disciplinary tool.

All of that is important, but it doesn't speak to Naaman's attitude, the point of focus for this chapter. As Naaman's character is introduced into the biblical narrative, we are given one more fact in 2 Kings 5:1: "but he was a leper."

At first glance, for those familiar with the Scriptures it is surprising to see a leper in such a public position: having access to the king and leading military units in battle. The surprise comes because we are so accustomed to seeing lepers in Israel being routinely ostracized and pushed away from those people who were not afflicted by the disease—all of which was done according to the laws of Moses.

The key, however, is that Israel had different rules about things like leprosy than did many of the surrounding nations. While Israel's lepers were normally isolated from non-lepers, this was not the custom in Syria/Aram. This leprosy, which in Israel would have excluded Naaman, didn't affect his participation in Syrian leadership.

Nevertheless, the disease degenerated its victims and eventually proved fatal. No cure for it was known. And this would have been an abiding concern leading to a definite desperation.

Knowing that his future was threatened by this fatal illness, Naaman was so desperate for a cure that he would, as we will see, take extreme measures to forestall its inevitable, inescapable conclusion. As it unfolds, the story will make it clear that Naaman is desperate—and that is the attitude he brings to these troubling circumstances.

Ben-hadad II: An Attitude of Concern

> Then the king of Aram said, "Go now, and I will send a letter to the king of Israel." He departed and took with him ten talents of silver and six thousand shekels of gold and ten changes of clothes. He brought the letter to the king of Israel, saying, "And now as this letter comes to you, behold, I have sent Naaman my servant to you, that you may cure him of his leprosy." (2 Kings 5:5–6)

Have you ever had a friend? I don't mean an acquaintance or neighbor or coworker. I mean a real friend. The kind of friend you would do anything for. A friend you would make any sacrifice for. A friend for whom you would do whatever it takes to help. Have you ever had a friend . . . like *that*?

Jesus spoke of this very thing when He said, "Greater love has no one than this, that one lay down his life for his friends" (John 15:13). He said it as He was preparing to go to the cross and do that very thing for His friends. That kind of rare and treasured friend doesn't come around every day. But King Ben-hadad II was that kind of friend to Naaman.

Through a series of circumstances, Naaman becomes aware that in Israel (enemy territory!) there is a prophet who could bring relief and even recovery to his disease. Naaman's immediate response is to go to the king, who respects and admires this general. And when presented with what might be an opportunity for his friend and general to be healed, the king takes drastic measures!

What were they?

First, the king of Syria drafts a letter to his hated enemy, Jehoram the king of Israel, asking him to come to his aid. This would have been a remarkable act of humility for Ben-hadad. Let's face it, none of us enjoys going to someone with whom we have had problems and admitting that we need his or her help. It feels embarrassing. It makes us vulnerable. We are exposed before someone who could very well use our vulnerability against us. It is an action filled with risk. Yet such is the concern of the king for his friend that he willingly humbles himself before his greatest foe to seek his help.

Second, Ben-hadad puts his money where his mouth is, and he does it in lavish style! In addition to the letter, the king backs up his concern with "ten talents of silver and six thousand shekels of gold and ten changes of clothes." The ten changes of clothes are pretty self-explanatory, but what about the gold and silver? How much is Ben-hadad willing to invest in his general's well-being?

To unravel that question, we must first remember that in ancient times money didn't come in denominations, but rather it was dispensed in weight. How do we know that? *The Bible Knowledge Commentary* says that Naaman was given "10 talents (ca. 750 pounds) of silver, 600 shekels (ca. 150 pounds) of gold." In today's money, that would translate into over $190,000 in silver and over $3.27 million in gold. Literally, a king's ransom! The talents and shekels in question are what amounts to wagonloads of gold and silver.

If it is true that you can discover what people really care about by observing how they spend their money, Ben-hadad's values are clearly presented. His attitude of concern for his friend is so intense that he is willing to part with almost $3.5 million of his monetary reserves if it might bring deliverance to Naaman. What a wonderful, gracious attitude!

Jehoram: An Attitude of Despair

He brought the letter to the king of Israel, saying, "And now as this letter comes to you, behold, I have sent Naaman my servant to you, that you may cure him of his leprosy." When the king of Israel read the letter, he tore his clothes and said, "Am I God, to kill and to make alive, that this man is sending word to me to cure a man of his leprosy? But consider now, and see how he is seeking a quarrel against me." (2 Kings 5:6–7)

One of the tragic realities of Israel's ancient divided kingdom was the poor quality of their kings. While the Southern Kingdom of Judah would have the occasional reformer king who would destroy the high places of idol worship and call the people back to worshipping and serving the God of Abraham, Isaac, and Jacob, the Northern Kingdom of Israel had no such "good" kings. The repeated litany that these northern kings "did evil in the sight of the Lord" not only underlines the spiritual condition of the nation but also sets the stage for the attitude of Jehoram, the king of Israel.

First, we can only imagine the wave of turbulence that rippled through Israel's capital city of Samaria when Naaman, the Syrian general responsible for heaping so much defeat on their nation, waltzed boldly into enemy territory leading wagons of gold and silver (which no doubt meant he was also accompanied by troops to protect such wealth). Naaman's presence in the capital was not simply bold or daring, it was threatening. And Jehoram felt that threat deeply.

Any insecurities sent buzzing around in Jehoram's mind by Naaman's arrival would have only been exacerbated upon reading Ben-hadad's letter to him. The letter is clear—the king of Aram expected the king of Israel to see to it that Naaman, the Syrian army captain, was healed of a fatal disease for which there was no cure. No wonder Jehoram's attitude is one of despair! Listen to the anguished cry he makes upon reading the letter:

> Am I God, to kill and to make alive, that this man is sending word to me to cure a man of his leprosy? But consider now, and see how he is seeking a quarrel against me (v. 7).

It's fascinating that Jehoram would invoke the name of God in his lament since, like all the northern kings, he had no relationship with Israel's true God. Jehoram rightly measures the size of the task and sees himself as inadequate for it. However, that inadequacy was not enough to motivate him to turn to God—who Jehoram seems to acknowledge *is* capable of healing Naaman's leprosy. He affirms that God is able "to make alive," which, in Naaman's case, means lifting the condition of death that he carries in his diseased body.

Jehoram's attitude of despair is plain to see—but its root cause is more subtle. Because he has no relationship with God, the king of Israel has no resources beyond himself. Since he can only do what he can only do, he knows that he can't do what his enemy, Ben-hadad, has requested—and in the process, he smells a rat. Rather than turning to God and becoming the kind of king the people desperately needed, Jehoram sees Ben-hadad's request through the dark lenses of cynicism and ascribes sinister motives to his enemy: "See how he is seeking a quarrel against me" (v. 7).

Jehoram sees the situation as impossible, and he concludes that this is all a ruse. Ben-hadad, he proposes, has set up an impossible challenge so that when Jehoram inevitably fails Syria will have an excuse to attack Israel. What makes this such an unfortunate assumption is that we have already seen Ben-hadad's motives, and they seem clearly born out of concern for his friend, not out of a desire to torment his enemy.

Jehoram's despair can only see the bleakness of unavoidable failure—and his attitude of despair and grief (pictured by the tearing of his garments) will leak out of the palace and become known among his people—people he is spiritually unfit to lead.

Elisha: An Attitude of Availability

It happened when Elisha the man of God heard that the king of Israel had torn his clothes, that he sent word to the king, saying, "Why have you torn your clothes? Now let him come to me, and he shall know that there is a prophet in Israel." (2 Kings 5:8)

Although Elisha is the main character in this book, he has only a brief cameo appearance in this critical event, yet that appearance would prove to be transformative. Notice how his response to Naaman's plight differs from King Jehoram's. Having heard of the king's gesture of grief (the torn garments), he makes himself available once more, immediately offering his assistance.

How does he offer to help? First, he questions the king's dramatic gesture—a gesture that would be unnecessary if Jehoram truly knew the God he had so long ignored. But more importantly, the prophet welcomes Naaman to come to him and find help. Elisha is available. He says: "Now let him come to me, and he shall know that there is a prophet in Israel" (v. 8).

Here it is important to remember the role of a prophet in Israel. He was there to represent God before the people. When Elisha says, "Then he will know that there is a prophet in Israel," it is not a "check me out" moment of ego and pride. The fact that there is a prophet in Israel bears witness to the greater truth that there was a God in Israel—whether the people or their king acknowledged Him or not. Elisha's invitation to Naaman was not so that the Syrian leader could experience Elisha's greatness but rather the greatness of Elisha's God.

It is also helpful to remember that up to this point Elisha's service has been limited to the people of Israel. However, almost as if he intuits that there is a larger, better story in play, the prophet does not hesitate to extend grace to an outsider. A foreigner. A Gentile. The enemy.

This is radically countercultural thinking in his generation. It would remain countercultural eight hundred years later when Jesus started His ministry to the "lost sheep of the house of Israel" (Matthew 15:24) and then expanded the mission by sending His followers to the "uttermost part of the earth" (Acts 1:8 KJV). Paul would pick up the banner and carry it forward, declaring the message of grace to be not only for the Jews but also for the Gentiles (Romans 1:16). The foreigner. The outsider.

Elisha was eight hundred years ahead of his time, but he was in perfect rhythm with the heart of the God who loves the world.

This warm and wonderful invitation from Elisha the prophet to Naaman the enemy, however, would surprise the captain, who is unprepared for the manner in which the promised help will be provided.

Naaman (Part Two); An Attitude of Indignation

So Naaman came with his horses and his chariots and stood at the doorway of the house of Elisha. Elisha sent a messenger to him, saying, "Go and wash in the Jordan seven times, and your flesh will be restored to you and you will be clean." But Naaman was furious and went away and said, "Behold, I thought, 'He will surely come out to me and stand and call on the name of the LORD his God, and wave his hand over the place and cure the leper.' Are not Abanah and Pharpar, the rivers of Damascus, better than all the waters of Israel?

Could I not wash in them and be clean?" So he turned and went away in a rage.

Then his servants came near and spoke to him and said, "My father, had the prophet told you to do some great thing, would you not have done it? How much more then, when he says to you, 'Wash, and be clean'?" So he went down and dipped himself seven times in the Jordan, according to the word of the man of God; and his flesh was restored like the flesh of a little child and he was clean. (2 Kings 5:9–14)

Naaman's words tell us what he was expecting:

Behold, I thought, "He will surely come out to me and stand and call on the name of the LORD his God, and wave his hand over the place and cure the leper." (v. 11)

Instead, Naaman got a rather rude awakening. Elisha doesn't even come to him; instead, he sends his servant with a message. Additionally, what that servant said was clearly not what Naaman wanted to hear. What were those instructions? *The Expositor's Bible Commentary* offers:

Elisha's instructions to Naaman reflect the general procedure for healing leprosy (Leviticus 14:7–9), although the specific details are different. The command for Naaman to bathe seven times in the Jordan River may approximate the sevenfold sprinkling administered by the priest. The number seven occurs frequently in the regulations in Leviticus 13–14, probably symbolizing the completeness of the healing process—and the restoration to wholeness that was the leper's primary need.

As we have seen, Naaman obviously expected to be received with respect. He anticipated some pomp and circumstance, and he expected that some distinctive act of healing would be performed. He did not expect to be sent to the muddy, and actually rather unimpressive, Jordan River. After all, there were some pretty amazing rivers available back home in Aram—why not go there instead? Instead, he "went away in a rage" (v. 12). Why? *The Bible Knowledge Commentary* paints the picture for us:

> Naaman turned from Elisha's house angry for two reasons: (1) His pride had been offended by Elisha's offhanded treatment of him; he had expected a cleansing ceremony in keeping with his own dignity. (2) He resented having been told to wash in a muddy river that he considered inferior to the . . . rivers in his hometown; the water of the Jordan, he thought, could not possibly do him any good.

Naaman's outrage, however, was not shared by his servants, who saw the request very differently. Notice:

> Then his servants came near and spoke to him and said, "My father, had the prophet told you to do some great thing, would you not have done it? How much more then, when he says to you, 'Wash, and be clean'?" (v. 13)

Again, *The Bible Knowledge Commentary* frames it well, "What harm would there be in giving his remedy a try?

Undoubtedly feeling rather ashamed Naaman humbled himself and obeyed the word of the Lord. As he obeyed in faith he was cleansed. God did even more for him and restored his flesh to its soft boyhood texture."

This is remarkable for two reasons. First, the healing occurred when Naaman humbled himself to accept Elisha's instructions. This lines up with a repeated theme in the Scriptures that humility is a key ingredient to our relationship with God (emphasis added):

- Psalm 10:17: "O LORD, You have heard the desire of the *humble*; You will strengthen their heart."
- Matthew 11:29: "Take My yoke upon you and learn from Me, for I am gentle and *humble* in heart, and you will find rest for your souls."
- James 4:6: "But He gives a greater grace. Therefore it says, 'God is opposed to the proud, but gives grace to the *humble*.'"
- James 4:10: "*Humble* yourselves in the presence of the Lord, and He will exalt you."
- 1 Peter 3:8: "To sum up, all of you be harmonious, sympathetic . . . kindhearted, and *humble* in spirit."
- 1 Peter 5:5: "You younger men, likewise, be subject to your elders; and all of you, clothe yourselves with *humility* toward one another, for God is opposed to the proud, but gives grace to the humble."
- 1 Peter 5:6: "Therefore *humble* yourselves under the mighty hand of God, that He may exalt you at the proper time."

Naaman's willingness to humble himself—first to the counsel of his servants, then to the simple instructions of Elisha, and ultimately to the Lord's provision—made the difference in his life, and he was healed. While Israel was bowing to the false idols of the surrounding cultures, Naaman, the Syrian pagan, was learning to bow before the God of Abraham, Isaac, and Jacob.

The second remarkable thing is the initial source of hope that Naaman had been offered. As you may have noticed, we skipped an unnamed but rather significant player on the stage of this drama—and her attitude may be the most enlightening of all. Let's return to the outset of the chapter.

A Servant Girl: An Attitude of Compassion for Her Enemy

> Now the Arameans had gone out in bands and had taken captive a little girl from the land of Israel; and she waited on Naaman's wife. She said to her mistress, "I wish that my master were with the prophet who is in Samaria! Then he would cure him of his leprosy." Naaman went in and told his master, saying, "Thus and thus spoke the girl who is from the land of Israel." (2 Kings 5:2–4)

Who is your worst enemy? Nationally, you might answer that question one way and personally you might answer it a very different way. One of the problems with enemies, however, especially worst enemies, is that it is hard to make yourself wish them well. It feels much more natural (and satisfying) to want to see them suffer in some way because of whatever harm they have done (or appeared to do) to us.

When I was growing up, my country's worst enemy was the Soviet Union. As a result, we cheered against them in the Olympics, wanted to beat them to the moon, and were taught to believe that any calamity that befell them was deserved.

As an adult, however, I found myself traveling repeatedly to Russia—and meeting some of the most wonderful people I have ever known. It made me realize afresh that I had drawn the circle of relationships too tightly and that I needed to learn how to reach beyond my comfort zones to those who fell outside my criteria for defining who were and who were not "good people."

This, of course, is a learning exercise about more clearly representing the heart of Jesus—who reached out to a Samaritan woman, Roman centurions, a Canaanite woman, and others who were ethnically outside the accepted norms of Jewish thinking. And His heart is presented in this ancient story by a most surprising character.

Remember, in addition to being a leper, Naaman was a warrior who had led Syria's armies against Israel. When you read 1 and 2 Kings, you find that Syria and Israel were going at each other constantly (see 1 Samuel 30:8; 2 Kings 13:21; 2 Kings 24:2). There were seasons of respite, to be sure, but clearly one of Israel's most consistent opponents was Syria—and part of the evidence of this is that Naaman had taken a little girl captive during one of Syria's many incursions across the border of Israel. The Israelite girl was now a servant to Naaman's wife, and she was the one who directed his attention to Elisha, the prophet of Israel, as the person who could remove his leprosy.

That is pretty astounding when you remember that this girl is a slave because Naaman had attacked her country, had won the victory, and had taken her as a captive. Imagine the pain and heartache of this young girl as she was ripped from her home, her family, and her village and enslaved in a foreign land—serving the wife of the very man who had stolen her. She would have had plenty of reason for anger, bitterness, or revenge.

Yet, in spite of that, she showed concern and compassion, and sought Naaman's good—reaching beyond her own pain and loss to offer him healing from his leprosy. *The New Bible Commentary* says, "The simple faith of the servant girl that Elisha would be able to cure Naaman's disease was in stark contrast to the reaction of the king of Israel. His panic (v. 7) is almost comical and full of irony. The king could not exercise God's power over life and death, but it did not occur to him to send Naaman to the man of God who could."

"Love your enemies, do good to those who hate you." –Jesus (Luke 6:27)

Although this event occurred hundreds of years before the coming of Christ, this Jewish girl and the prophet Elisha display hearts that anticipate the teaching of Jesus: Love your enemies.

"But I say to you, love your enemies and pray for those who persecute you." (Matthew 5:44)

"But I say to you who hear, love your enemies, do good to those who hate you." (Luke 6:27)

"But love your enemies, and do good, and lend, expecting nothing in return; and your reward will be great, and you will be sons of the Most High; for He Himself is kind to ungrateful and evil men." (Luke 6:35)

The servant girl foreshadows the heart of Jesus, who was constantly reaching beyond. He reached to Gentiles, Samaritans, tax collectors, prostitutes, and, yes, lepers to show that His rescuing love was not limited to the religious. His mercy and grace were not the sole preserve of the insiders and the accepted.

Jesus's point was that though the nation of Israel had learned to love their friends and hate their enemies, they needed to discover higher ground—loving with the heart of the Father who loves all of us, even though we had all made ourselves His enemies. Like the Jewish servant girl in Naaman's household, Israel needed to reach beyond and see the love of God that would embrace the entire world. Why? Jesus.

We have seen and testify that the Father has sent the Son to be the Savior of the world. (1 John 4:14)

So how do we wind this down? It is interesting that Elijah is mentioned twenty-nine times in the New Testament. By contrast, Elisha is named in the New Testament only once. By Jesus. About this incident.

And there were many lepers in Israel in the time of Elisha the prophet; and none of them was cleansed, but only Naaman the Syrian. (Luke 4:27)

Matthew Henry wrote, "Our Savior's miracles were intended for the lost sheep of the house of Israel, yet one, like a crumb, fell from the table to a woman of Canaan; so this one miracle Elisha wrought for Naaman, a Syrian; for God does good to all, and will have all men to be saved."

That is still true today. And what Naaman experienced physically is available to all spiritually in Christ because Jesus, like Elisha and the Jewish servant girl, reaches beyond—He reaches to whoever will come to Him by faith. It is Jesus's attitude of perfect grace that draws us to His cleansing power, as described in the words of James L. Nicholson's song:

> Lord Jesus, I long to be perfectly whole;
> I want Thee forever to live in my soul;
> Break down every idol, cast out every foe—
> Now wash me, and I shall be whiter than
>   snow.
> Whiter than snow, yes, whiter than snow,
> Now wash me, and I shall be whiter than
>   snow.

5

THE END . . .
AND BEYOND

I was in the seventh grade and eleven years old when my English teacher announced to our class that President John F. Kennedy had just been assassinated. That sunny November Friday ushered in what were arguably the darkest days the United States had experienced since Pearl Harbor's "date which will live in infamy." Those were days that would be unparalleled by any other event until, perhaps, the terror attacks on September 11, 2001.

To this day, more than five decades later, I remember so much.

I remember the sight of the mourners lined up for blocks outside the capitol rotunda where the slain president lay in state.

I remember the seemingly endless weekend that felt as if it would drag on forever.

I remember the stark, gray images on our black and white television of uniformed military personnel standing vigil over the casket of their dead commander-in-chief.

I remember the sound of the mournful drums marking cadence for the funeral procession, as a soldier in dress uniform led a riderless horse in the funeral procession—symbolic of the fallen leader of the nation.

I remember the pain I felt as a boy seeing little John-John Kennedy (JFK's toddler son) standing by the street, saluting the caisson that carried his father's casket to its final resting place in Arlington National Cemetery.

The mourning, grief, and sense of loss of that brutal weekend and beyond was felt across racial, social, economic, and even, to some degree, political lines. On November 22, the life of the nation's leader had been brutally snuffed out, and the days of grief would go unassuaged. Such is the pain of a people when a significant figure or leader or person is lost—and that is not just a modern phenomenon. Such was also the pain of Israel's King Jehoash as he contemplated the death of the prophet Elisha—which we read about in 2 Kings 13.

This is the circumstance as we return to the story, and as we do, we return our focus to Elisha—who has been noticeably absent from the narrative since the beginning of chapter 9. Having served as the prophet of the land of Israel for more than sixty years, Elisha is approaching death. And Jehoash, the king, comes to grieve and lament the coming loss of this important figure.

A Lament for the Dying

> Now Elisha had been suffering from the illness from which he died. Jehoash king of Israel went down to see him and wept over him. "My father! My father!" he cried. "The chariots and horsemen of Israel!" (2 Kings 13:14 NIV)

Journalist and adventurer Ernest Hemingway wrote, "Every true story ends in death." That statement is irrefutably true, except, as we will see, when it isn't. Elisha's true story now reaches that inevitable conclusion, and the beginning of his ending is a moment that both compares and contrasts with the earlier departure of Elisha's mentor, Elijah.

- **Contrast:** Notice that verse 14 makes it clear that Elisha contracted some undefined terminal illness, and he would eventually succumb to it. By contrast, Elijah left this life for the next without passing through the veil of death. In fact, Elijah was one of two people recorded in Scripture (along with Enoch; see Genesis 5:24) to avoid death—defying the logic of Hemingway's seemingly foolproof assertion about death. When placed in contrast with Elijah's dramatic living exit, Elisha's death looks positively ordinary.

- **Comparison:** While Elijah and Elisha would experience very different departures from this life, the king here utters the exact same lament that Elisha had himself declared at Elijah's leaving. Both Elisha and King

Jehoash said, "My father! My father! The chariots and horsemen of Israel! (2 Kings 2:12; 13:14). Calling Elisha "My father!" was a remarkable display of humility and respect from the king, and as *The Bible Knowledge Commentary* suggests, "By the phrase 'the chariots and horsemen of Israel' he showed that he recognized in Elisha, and behind him in the Lord, the real defense and power of Israel against all her adversaries."

If we are correct that Jehoash's words form a lament that the true power and security of Israel was passing along with the prophet, this is an extraordinary admission coming from the king who is supposed to be that very protector of the nation. Remember again the roles of the three main offices in Israel:

- The prophet was to represent God before the people.
- The priest was to represent the people before God.
- The king was to administer the government, arbitrate disagreements, and—of critical importance here—lead the armies in defense of the nation.

The king—the defender of the nation—contemplates the imminent passing of the prophet, Elisha, and sees the nation as having been left utterly defenseless. In both the case of the comparison and the case of the contrast, however, there is the unmistakable echo of fear, insecurity, and emptiness that should lead to the great reminder of the true Protector of His people—God himself.

This anxiety echoed the sentiment of Isaiah the prophet. In Isaiah 6 we read:

> In the year of King Uzziah's death I saw the Lord sitting on a throne, lofty and exalted, with the train of His robe filling the temple. (Isaiah 6:1)

What is the connection? Under Uzziah, the people of God had experienced real stability and peace. *Easton's Bible Dictionary* says that, with the exception of Jehoshaphat, Uzziah's fifty-two-year reign was the most prosperous since the time of Solomon. In the same way, in both Uzziah and Elisha's departures, with such a season of relative calm and stability coming to an end, the emotional questions bubbling to the surface would have been:

What now?
Who will watch over us?
Who will protect us?
Who will lead us?
Who will provide for us?

Isaiah's vision of the Lord on His throne is a very dramatic corrective to those fears. Who would care for them? The same God who had brought them out of Egypt, into the land, and safely to that day. The picture of the living God "lofty and exalted" (Isaiah 6:1) was the answer to Isaiah's anxiety over the loss of Israel's significant leader and king.

Like the people of Isaiah's day at the passing of Uzziah, Jehoash needed to look higher, as he will have to do at the eventual passing of Elisha. He needed to look beyond the prophet of God to the God of the prophet. The true Provider of our needs and lives.

Jehoash needed to look to the living God instead of human leaders, governments, or prophets as his source and resource. That was certainly the emphasis of hymnwriter Maltbie D. Babcock who in 1901 affirmed:

> This is my Father's world.
> O let me ne'er forget
> That though the wrong seems oft so
>   strong,
> God is the Ruler yet.
> This is my Father's world: why should my
>   heart be sad?
> The Lord is King; let the heavens ring!
> God reigns; let earth be glad!

Babcock knew what Jehoash needed to know—and what we need to remember in our own times of uncertainty and instability. We can trust in the protection and power of our God when human resources have been exhausted.

A Lament for the Kingdom

Elisha said to him, "Take a bow and arrows." So he took a bow and arrows. Then he said to the king of Israel, "Put your hand on the bow." And he put his hand on it, then Elisha laid his hands on the king's hands. He said, "Open the window toward the east," and he opened it. Then Elisha said, "Shoot!" And he shot. And he said, "The LORD's arrow of victory, even the arrow of victory over Aram; for you will defeat the

Arameans at Aphek until you have destroyed them."
Then he said, "Take the arrows," and he took them.
And he said to the king of Israel, "Strike the ground,"
and he struck it three times and stopped. So the man
of God was angry with him and said, "You should
have struck five or six times, then you would have
struck Aram until you would have destroyed it. But
now you shall strike Aram only three times." (2 Kings
13:15–19)

Now, I have to admit that this just sounds weird. It seems
as if Jehoash had done exactly as he had been instructed
by Elisha. In fact, he struck the ground three times when
the implied instruction was to simply strike the ground.
Period. One strike would seem to have been enough. So,
why is Elisha suddenly enraged at the shaken king?

One of the more helpful books I have read in recent
years—and I have read it at least five times—is *Misreading
Scripture with Western Eyes*. The authors, Randy Richards
and Brandon O'Brien, challenge those of us in the West
to understand that the Bible was written in an Eastern
culture with a very different set of presuppositions and
a very different cultural backdrop than western cultures
(like mine) normally value. The upshot of this fact is that
every time we open the Bible we are entering into a cross-
cultural experience.

As such, one of the realities of the cultural platform for
the Scriptures is found in what Richards and O'Brien call
"the things that are left unsaid." Throughout the pages
of the Scriptures, there seem to be missing pieces of in-
formation that we would benefit from. However, these

were things that the first hearers didn't need because those things were part of the accepted and understood fabric of their times and customs.

I would suggest that this is one of those times. There would, in the action of striking the ground with arrows, seem to have been some specific custom that was broadly known in their day but has been lost to the sands of time— erased by centuries of history and change. When ancient peoples would have heard of this event, they would most likely have nodded their heads with understanding. When we hear it, we scratch our heads in confusion. So, what can we make of it?

As he faces death, Elisha offers one more opportunity for the king to hear a message of hope. Perhaps moved by the grief of the king, Elisha mustered his strength to give Jehoash assurance that God would continue to stand by His people—even though they had not been standing with Him. *The New Bible Commentary* says:

> The story involves symbolic actions, as in the earlier miracle stories concerning Elisha. On this occasion, however, they were performed by the king (though Elisha placed his own hands over the king's when he fired the arrow; v. 16). Elisha's prophecy (17) confirms that the issue underlying this incident was Israel's survival of the Aramean oppression. The first action symbolized victory and recovery. However, the king's failure to perform the second action often enough determined that his success against Aram would be limited (19). It presumably signified a lack of faith or determination.

How did that work? In ancient times, hostilities were usually proclaimed by a messenger, king, or general making a public announcement of the start of combat by sending an arrow into the enemy's country or military base. Here, Elisha directed Jehoash to perform this as the first of two symbolic acts designed to anticipate the future victories that the Lord was promising to the king of Israel over the Syrians. Elisha's laying of his own hands upon the king's hands was apparently intended to represent the Lord's own power imparted to the symbolic arrow. As we have seen, the prophet was God's representative on earth, so his participation in the action symbolized God's involvement.

The king's shooting of the first arrow eastward—in the direction of the Syrian army's camp—was a declaration of war against them for invading Israel yet again. So far, so good.

That brings us to the second symbolic act. His striking the other arrows onto the ground was apparently in order to represent the number of victories he was hoping to gain. By stopping with the third however, Jehoash seemed to expose the weakness of his faith. Had he continued to strike the ground, he could have realized a thoroughly comprehensive victory over Israel's longstanding enemy. *The Bible Knowledge Commentary* affirms this perspective:

> God assured him that he would have victory by divine enablement. But perhaps Jehoash felt that God could not or would not do as much for him as Elisha implied. This unbelief explains why Elisha became angry. Jehoash had failed to trust God even though he knew what God had promised.

The event ends abruptly with Elisha's rebuke, leveled at the king's lack of confidence in God. It is an event filled with question marks and mystery for us, yet it is part of the biblical narrative because it connects what preceded (the king's lament over Elisha's soon passing) to the same reality that Isaiah discovered following the passing of Uzziah—Israel's security was not rooted in any prophet or king, but in the exalted God who had called the Israelites out of Egypt, named them the people of His own choice, and established them in the land they continued to inhabit. The lesson of the arrows was apparently intended by Elisha to cause Jehoash to lift his eyes to the God whose power was the real safety net for the nation.

This extraordinarily important truth for Israel is reinforced in Elisha's final mention in the Old Testament, found in the following verses. In my opinion at least, this may be the weirdest story found anywhere in Israel's Scriptures.

A Life for the Dead

Elisha died, and they buried him. Now the bands of the Moabites would invade the land in the spring of the year. As they were burying a man, behold, they saw a marauding band; and they cast the man into the grave of Elisha. And when the man touched the bones of Elisha he revived and stood up on his feet. (2 Kings 13:20–22)

Is it just me or does this seem really strange? It has more of the sound and feel of a legend rather than a true, biblical story—yet here it is. But why is it here? What is its point? And what does it have to do with the two stories that precede it? Before trying to unravel those questions, let's visualize the event with a little biblical imagination.

Because winter rains annually made ancient roads largely impassable, military campaigns would begin in the spring when conditions were more favorable for moving military personnel and supplies. This is clearly stated in 2 Samuel 11:1, "Then it happened in the spring, at the time when kings go out to battle . . ." It is the spring of the year as the story opens, Elisha has been dead for about a year (as we will later see), and the Moabites are launching an attack on Israel. What happens next feels almost random.

After describing Jehoash's event with the arrows and telling us that it was spring and the season for a return of Moabite aggression, the narrator, in what feels like a non sequitur, seems to switch tracks, saying: "As they were burying a man . . ." (v. 21).

Wait . . . what? Who are *they*? Who is this man? Where did this come from? A funeral procession of unnamed people is carrying the dead body of an unnamed man toward an unnamed place for burial. So what? Again, this text almost screams that something here is being left unsaid. Nevertheless, the story continues with these questions left unanswered by saying that as they proceed to the burial site a Moabite raiding party is spotted off in the distance. The response of the pallbearers? They look for the first grave available (probably one of the many caves used by ancient Jews for burial), and it just happens to be the grave in which the now long-dead Elisha is entombed. Coincidence? I think not.

In a moment of panic, they toss the body into the grave and take off running for town. However, to the surprise of everyone—not least of all the dead man, or should we say the *formerly* dead man—the corpse lands on Elisha's bones and is brought back to life! In my imagination, I see this dead man jump from the tomb and upon seeing the Moabite raiders closing in on him, he takes off running as he yells to the pallbearers, "Hey, fellas, wait for me!"

One detail here, by the way, explains how we know Elisha has been dead for a year. Ancient Jewish burial practices involved the careful wrapping of the corpse in cloth, binding various spices and ointments against the body, as we see in the record of Jesus's burial in the New Testament. This package—body and all—would be placed in a tomb so that all of the fleshy parts of the body could deteriorate and disappear, leaving only the bones— a process that took about a year. The bones would then be retrieved, placed in an ossuary (a bone box), and secured permanently in the family's crypt. Since the unnamed man's body landed on Elisha's bones rather than his body, the year-long process of deterioration was obviously complete.

That is all well and good, but let's not get caught in the weeds here. None of that should take our attention off the fact that Elisha's sixteenth and final miracle takes place after Elisha has been dead for a year! And that is the point.

This seemingly random event becomes the reader's "Isaiah 6 moment." Why? The simple reality is that, even though Elisha is dead, God is not. The same God Isaiah saw high and lifted up following Uzziah's death is still in control and doing mighty deeds even though his prophet, Elisha, is dead. Elisha may be dead, but the true and *living* God is alive and well—and actively involved in the affairs of this world.

Jehoash's lament that the nation would be bereft of help is answered by the help promised by the arrows and the evidence of a God who is not limited to human agencies to accomplish His purposes. It's a lesson for the people of that day—and ours as well.

The timeless, never-failing trustworthiness of our God is the important theme and lesson of 2 Kings 13, reminding us that our confidence is not to be in men and women who live and die, come and go, and are born and pass away. Our trust and hope are in the God whose power and presence are never diminished—whose eternity is the most real reality in the universe. As a result, where we choose to put our trust is of utmost importance.

This is why we would do well to be reminded of the wisdom of the Scriptures on this important subject:

> Do not trust in princes,
> In mortal man, in whom there is no
>   salvation.
>
> (Psalm 146:3)

> They will devour your harvest and your
>   food;
> They will devour your sons and your
>   daughters;
> They will devour your flocks and your
>   herds;

They will devour your vines and your fig
    trees;
They will demolish with the sword your
    fortified cities in which you trust.
                   (Jeremiah 5:17)

Woe to those who go down to Egypt for
    help
And rely on horses,
And trust in chariots because they are
    many
And in horsemen because they are very
    strong,
But they do not look to the Holy One of
    Israel, nor seek the LORD!
                   (Isaiah 31:1)

But . . .

Those who trust in the LORD
Are as Mount Zion, which cannot be
    moved but abides forever.
                 (Psalm 125:1)

When I am afraid,
I will put my trust in You.
             (Psalm 56:3)

Some trust in chariots, and some in horses;
But we will remember the name of the
    LORD our God.
                 (Psalm 20:7 NKJV)

When the days are darkest, our eyes, hearts, and prayers are to seek Him for solution. For help. For hope. No one else comes close. Nothing else will do. We go to Him—knowing that He never fails. He not only knows what is best but He is also capable of bringing it about.

As Isaac Watts's well-loved hymn says:

> O God, our help in ages past,
> Our hope for years to come,
> Our shelter from the stormy blast,
> And our eternal home.
>
> Under the shadow of Thy throne
> Thy saints have dwelt secure;
> Sufficient is Thine arm alone,
> And our defense is sure.

6

AN AVAILABLE LIFE
AND THE BIG STORY

As a boy, I only knew Marvel as the brand of comic books that I enjoyed less than DC Comics (the domain of Superman, Batman, and Wonder Woman). In 2008, however, Marvel did something utterly groundbreaking. Marvel Entertainment began one of the most ambitious movie-making projects of all time. With the release of *Iron Man,* a story began to unfold that would not be finally resolved until *Avengers: Endgame* in 2019. Along the way, a total of twenty-two films provided remarkable storytelling that existed at the micro-level with superheroes like Captain America, Thor, Spider-Man, Hulk, Black Panther, Ant-Man, Wasp, and many more joining Iron Man to form the Avengers. Each film had its own story filled with danger, action, and a bazillion dollars worth of special effects. Each film, in the micro, worked well as a stand-alone story. Each film had its own voice.

But there was also a macro-level of the story. All twenty-two movies provided the threads of a story arc that would eventually see the Avengers wage war with Thanos, the destroyer of life set on eradicating half the population of the universe. So, *Endgame* was not simply the name of the final film; it was the conclusion of the greater story being told in all the smaller individual stories. As fans of the Marvel Cinematic Universe exited the theaters by the millions, many talked about moments in *Endgame* that connected back to a Captain America moment in an earlier movie, or a scene in an earlier Thor movie, or some other connected dot from past MCU films. Those "reconnected dots," though innocuous at the time, suddenly burst into fresh new meaning—particularly when Iron Man/Tony Stark brought *Endgame* to its paramount moment with the exact same words that he used to close *Iron Man*—the very first film in this unbelievably complicated, brilliantly executed, and thoroughly captivating film project: "I am Iron Man." It was a masterstroke in cinematic storytelling.

At this point, the non-nerds among us may be wondering what the point of all of this is—so, let's get to it. While there has never been a film storytelling project of this complexity in the history of moviemaking, this type of multilayered approach is nothing new. In fact, we have been hinting at this all throughout this book.

This is essentially what the Bible is—a multilayered, interconnected set of stories that combine to tell one much bigger story. The big and ultimately eternal difference between the Bible's story and that of the MCU's tale is that the Bible story is both an absolutely true and infinitely more important story—the story of Jesus.

We often think of the Bible as one book—and that is vital. But that one book (comprised of sixty-six books) is ultimately woven together expertly by the heart and mind of God to tell one massive, eternal story. It's the story of the one true God, who loves His broken creation so much that He would move heaven and earth to rescue it. And along the way all of the "smaller stories" of the Bible fit into that great, redemptive story arc of Jesus and His cross and His resurrection. So we see God at work all throughout the Old Testament to tell the story that is truly Good News. Therefore we can see that:

Without losing any of its own significance or truthfulness, every "small" story in the Old Testament folds into and participates with the greatest story ever told: the story of Jesus.

- The exodus from Egypt anticipates Jesus's return from Egypt following Herod's threat in Matthew.
- The sacrifice for a cleansed leper in Leviticus anticipates Jesus's cleansing of a leper in Mark.
- A miracle of raising sons from the dead by Elijah and Elisha points forward to Jesus the Son being raised from the dead himself in Luke.
- A Passover lamb in Exodus points forward to the Lamb of God in John's gospel.

Dozens of examples could be offered, but the point is clear. Every story in the Old Testament is pointing forward, urging the reader to see the power of the moment while looking forward to a fuller, richer, truly divine fulfillment of that story. Without losing any of its own significance or truthfulness, every "small" story in the Old Testament folds into and participates with the greatest story ever told: the story of Jesus. Author Sally Lloyd-Jones puts it this way: "Every story whispers His name."

And this is where we once again consider our friend Elisha. He is a prime example of how a so-called small story (I think we have seen that Elisha's story is pretty big in its own right!) participates in the Bible's bigger, grander story.

And what we have seen so far in this book has been a not-so-subtle-attempt to repeatedly point out *how* the story of Elisha's available life points to the ultimate available life—the life of the Christ.

Three Ages of Miracles

We noted earlier that we sometimes have the impression that there are miracles on every page of the Bible, but remember, that isn't so. Every page is kissed with the miraculous by virtue of the fact that it is God-breathed, but miraculous moments are actually more scattered than continual.

In this way, at least, people living in Bible times lived very much as we do, in the day-to-day reality of life in a broken world. But that does not mean that the Bible is short of divine interventions; rather, they are largely grouped into three significant eras when God was doing something special in His world. Let's be reminded that these ages of miracles were the following:

Era One: The days of the Exodus
Era Two: The days of Elijah and Elisha
Era Three: The days of Jesus and His apostles

Within each these arenas of the miraculous, we also see a story of one person who prepares and the other who completes a specific mission. We see the reality of a forerunner and a finisher who, again, point forward and beyond themselves.

Era One: Moses in Preparation and Joshua in Fulfillment

Because Moses's story is so dramatically told that he covers four books of the Old Testament narrative, it's easy to forget that he did not finish the task he had been given. This is because the task had two parts:

- To lead the children of Israel *out* of their bondage in Egypt, and
- To lead the children of Israel *into* the land God had promised.

Obviously, Moses was God's instrument to achieve the first tasks, and in that regard Moses achieved remarkable things. Under God's hand, Moses did great miracles in Egypt—culminating with the parting of the Red Sea—to secure the liberation of the Hebrew slaves. Once out of

Egypt, he was given the task of presenting God's call to this massive extended family to become a nation where the unseen God would reign as their king. And Moses led Israel for forty years in the wilderness, bringing them to the very threshold of the Promised Land.

But his work ended there. Disciplined by God for a rash, angry, vindictive action in the wilderness—an action that ostensibly brought attention to himself rather than God (see Numbers 20:10)—Moses was disallowed from leading the people into the land to which they had journeyed so long. He was allowed to see it from a distance but not allowed to enter.

Joshua stepped into the unfinished work of his more celebrated forerunner, and he would lead them into their home. Under God's hand, Joshua would clear the land of enemies who would endanger the still-fledgling nation. Joshua completed the way that had been prepared by Moses. He would finish what the forerunner had begun.

Era Two: Elijah in Preparation and Elisha in Fulfillment

This, of course, is where most of our focus has been in this book. Elijah was the prophet selected by God to call His people back to himself—and he made a solid start to it. The decisive victory of Mount Carmel, however, would need continual underlining and reemphasis. When Elijah departed the scene, the work had begun—but was far from done.

As we have seen, in stepped Elisha. Not only did he continue the work of showing the people the proper wisdom of following God rather than pursuing the idols of the nations but he also completed the tasks of the two anointings that God had given to Elijah on Mount Horeb (see chapter one).

Again, the less-celebrated finisher (Elisha) completes work initially undertaken by his better-known forerunner (Elijah).

Era Three: John the Baptizer in Preparation and Jesus in Fulfillment

This final era of forerunner and finisher also finishes the story arc that the Scriptures have been establishing—yet with dramatic differences. Even in the telling of the story, we begin to see these three eras linked together in the big story of the Bible.

John the Baptizer was sent to be the actual forerunner of Jesus. This was part of the message of the angel Gabriel to John's father, Zacharias the priest:

> It is he who will go as a forerunner before Him in the spirit and power of Elijah, to turn the hearts of the fathers back to the children, and the disobedient to the attitude of the righteous, so as to make ready a people prepared for the Lord. (Luke 1:17)

Not coincidentally, this "forerunner" role was the antic-ipated fulfillment of an earlier forerunner, Elijah, described by Malachi with the very words that would close the Jew-ish (Old Testament) Scriptures:

> Behold, I am going to send you Elijah the prophet before the coming of the great and terrible day of the

LORD. He will restore the hearts of the fathers to their children and the hearts of the children to their fathers, so that I will not come and smite the land with a curse. (Malachi 4:5–6)

For some 450 years, the children of Israel looked for Elijah to come—no doubt feeding into a Jewish Passover custom that is still practiced today. The Passover seder includes a fifth cup of wine called "Elijah's cup." The wine is poured but is not drunk. It is left for Elijah in anticipation of the day when he would come to announce the arrival of Israel's long-awaited Messiah.

But "Elijah" has come. He came in the form of John the Baptizer of whom Jesus said: "And if you are willing to accept it, John himself is Elijah who was to come" (Matthew 11:14).

Tragically, the people of His day were not willing to accept it. As a result, not only did they miss "Elijah" but they also crucified their own Messiah. Yet, in that act of crucifixion was Jesus's great moment of completion. John's ministry had begun with the message: "Repent, for the kingdom of heaven is at hand" (Matthew 3:2).

Jesus repeated that message (Matthew 4:17) and then declared that He himself was the completion of that message when He claimed: "But if I cast out demons by the Spirit of God, then the kingdom of God has come upon you" (Matthew 12:28).

At His trials, Jesus exposed the nature of His kingdom ("not of this world," John 18:36) as He faced the deeply troubled Pilate and offered a place in that kingdom to a repentant thief dying at His side (Luke 23:42). Mostly, however, Jesus finished the work of the kingdom message by dying on the cross to make that kingdom available to those who deserved it least—among them, you and me. Paul wrote to the church at Colosse:

> For He rescued us from the domain of darkness, and transferred us to the kingdom of His beloved Son, in whom we have redemption, the forgiveness of sins. (Colossians 1:13–14)

How had Jesus accomplished such a transfer? Paul continued:

> For it was the Father's good pleasure for all the fullness to dwell in Him, and through Him to reconcile all things to Himself, having made peace through the blood of His cross; through Him, I say, whether things on earth or things in heaven. (Colossians 1:19–20)

On the cross. There, the story that was woven throughout the Scriptures found its fullness of meaning. There, our sins were atoned. There, adoption into the family of God was made possible. There, the rebellious were restored. There, the story reached its climax. The truest and best endgame of all.

Forerunners and finishers. A story so beautifully woven together that it takes our breath away not only in its telling but also in its purpose—the rescue of fallen human beings who, despite being fallen are the shocking objects of God's great love.

Forerunners and finishers.

And one seemingly insignificant detail becomes the thread that runs throughout the Bible. As we see in Jonah 2:9, "Salvation is from the LORD." This eternal reality became both Jesus's stated mission and His prophesied purpose:

- **Stated mission.** "For the Son of Man has come to seek and to save that which was lost." (Luke 19:10)
- **Prophesied Purpose.** "You shall call His name Jesus, for He will save His people from their sins." (Matthew 1:21)

I put those two texts out of chronological order for a reason. The three finishers of the biblical story of forerunners and finishers have something in common beside being finishers in their particular stories. They share a name…

Joshua (Heb. *Yeshua*): "Yah (or Yahweh) saves"

Elisha (Heb. *Elisha*): "My God (or El, Elohim) is my salvation"

Jesus (Heb. *Yeshua*): "Yah (or Yahweh) saves"

Not only did these the figures share missions as finishers but they also shared names that reflect the ultimate truth— that it is God who saves. God alone. No other. Joshua and Elisha move the biblical story forward to see:

- The ultimate expression of God's rescue.
- The ultimate expression of God's story.
- The ultimate Finisher—Jesus Christ, the Lamb of God who came to take away the sins of the world (John 1:29).

So, it should be no surprise to us that the ultimate Finisher, as He was completing the work of our rescue on the cross, would declare:

It is finished. (John 19:30)

In these pages, we have studied the available life of Elisha, and we have seen how God used him in his generation. But we also have observed his available life pointing forward to the ultimate available life—the One who willingly came to this world, took on himself the flesh of humanity, and revealed the heart of His Father to us. The ultimate available life that, having completed its mission, causes Jesus to be described as, "the author and finisher of our faith" (Hebrews 12:2; NKJV).

> *God took Elisha's available life and used it as a beacon to point forward to Christ.*

Like all foreshadowings, Elisha himself is not the solution. The danger of such anticipation is that it often yields the bitter fruit of disappointment. Elisha was God's provision for the moment, but he could never be the full provision of the Father for the needs of His own any more than Joshua could before him.

That full provision would only be realized in the one true Provision—Jesus. God took Elisha's available life and used it as a beacon to point forward to Christ—the one who came to live up to His name, which means "The Lord saves."

And in a way similar to the way God used the faithful Elisha, He can likewise use us—to point backward to the

Christ. This can happen if we will likewise be available to His perfect purposes. Living as followers of Christ and carrying forward His finished work.

> Lifted up was He to die;
> "It is finished!" was His cry;
> Now in Heav'n exalted high.
> Hallelujah! What a Savior!

"HERE AM I . . . SEND ME"

Different books are written for different reasons.
Some are to entertain; others are to inform.
Some are to challenge; others are to educate.
Some are to enlighten; others to present facts.

This book is intended to elicit a response. From you, the reader, and from me, the writer.

Arguably, the larger lesson of Elisha's life is that we might understand what God can do with an available heart. The question for us to wrestle with is whether or not we will likewise be available for His work. To that end, one of my favorite little books is Jill Briscoe's delightful reflection on the Exodus story, entitled *Here Am I—Send Aaron*. When first encountering God, Moses was not all that available.

He was happy to sit on the sidelines and show none of the instant willingness to become an instrument in the hands of His God that we have seen in Elisha. But as we know, Moses eventually got on board, and the rest, as they say, is history.

> *We have the opportunity to respond to the call for an available life in our own generation.*

In the same way, our God desires to use us to point people to the Savior their hearts long for— even though they don't know they are actually longing for Him. The response called for is the answer of the overwhelmed Isaiah in the throne room of God, "Here am I. Send me!" (Isaiah 6:8), as the prophet declared himself available to God.

In this book we have considered the life of Elisha, who when confronted with the prophetic mantle of Elijah, picked it up, looked to the heavens, and declared, "Where is the LORD, the God of Elijah?" (2 Kings 2:14)—making himself available to represent God to the people of his own times.

Now we have the opportunity to respond to the call for an available life in our own generation. How will we respond?

"Here am I . . . send me."

Help us get the word out!

Our Daily Bread Publishing exists to feed the soul with the Word of God.

If you appreciated this book, please let others know.

- Pick up another copy to give as a gift.
- Share a link to the book or mention it on social media.
- Write a review on your blog, on a bookseller's website, or at our own site (odb.org/store).
- Recommend this book for your church, book club, or small group.

Connect with us:

 @ourdailybread

 @ourdailybread

 @ourdailybread

Our Daily Bread Publishing
PO Box 3566
Grand Rapids, Michigan 49501 USA

 books@odb.org